ONE-POT
Vegetarian
Dishes

Amy Cotler

A John Boswell Associates/King Hill Productions Book

HarperCollins*Publishers*

FIRST EDITION

Designed by Stephanie Tevonian

Library of Congress Cataloging-in-Publication Data

Cotler, Amy.
    One-pot vegetarian dishes / Amy Cotler. —1st ed.
        p.   cm.
    "A John Boswell Associates/King Hill Productions book."
    Includes index.
    ISBN 0-06-017319-X
    1. Vegetarian cookery.   2. Entrées (Cookery)   I. Title.
TX897.C667   1996
641.5'636—dc20   96-4115

96 97 98 99 00 HC 10 9 8 7 6 5 4 3 2 1

For
Tommy and Emma, my two top tasters.

A warm thank you to my mom, my friends, and all my students at Peter Kump's School of Culinary Arts, who cooked these recipes for friends and family.

Contents

Introduction: Eating Vegetarian

The recipes in this book are designed to put fresh, tasty dinners on your family table fast. The fact that these particular recipes are all vegetarian—that is, contain no meat—is incidental. Because vegetarian eating isn't just for vegetarians anymore. Did you know that presently half of all American households eat at least two vegetarian dinners a week? Over twenty percent eat four or more meatless meals. The numbers are growing every day, and it's easy to see why.

Most vegetables are practically fat-free, and they contain no cholesterol. Besides providing healthy nutrition and excellent eating, vegetables are colorful, tasty, versatile, easy to prepare, quick to cook, and a relative bargain at the supermarket. For, of course, it is vegetables, grains, and beans that provide the bases for most vegetarian cooking. If you are not strict—and I am not—they can be augmented with a bit of cheese or other milk products and occasionally a little egg.

But don't forget the "one-pot" that clinches this collection. The idea is simple: cook a complete meal in one pot, for less shopping, less cleanup, and more fun. Don't worry about menu planning. These meal-in-one suppers stand on their own. Just add some bread and sometimes a salad and invite your friends over for an effortless dinner that's right up to date.

As a working mom, I found these recipes a road map to midweek supper sanity, a way to enjoy an easy homemade dinner with my family but still provide healthy fresh food. As a cooking teacher, I truly enjoyed the challenge of serving up delicious vegetarian meals in exciting and unexpected ways. I adore playing with a multitude of international cuisines, and you'll see some of their influences here in recipes like Moroccan Tomatoes Stuffed with Eggplant, Indonesian Green Beans and Tofu in Peanut Sauce, and Spicy South Indian Vegetable Curry. While the ingredients called for are common, the results most decidedly are not.

These economical meals range from Portobello Mushroom Lasagna and Texas Tortilla Pie to Broccoli Stir-Fry with Black Bean Sauce and Savory Corn Pudding with Tomato Salsa, from a hot and hearty Vegetable Cobbler to cool and silky Szechuan Cold Sesame Noodles. There are soups and stews, pizzas and pastas, frittatas and fritters. It may take you a little while to get used to the lightness of vegetarian dining, but it's an adjustment you're sure to enjoy. Remember, you don't have to get all your protein and nutrients in a single meal. What's important is the overall balance of your diet.

Before you start creating these dishes, note that each chapter focuses on meals prepared in a different pot—but one pot. All the pots used are typical kitchen tools; standard saucepans, stew pots (which might be a Dutch oven or an enameled flameproof casserole), skillets, a wok, a steamer, a large baking sheet. The pasta pot and soup pot called for could just as well be a large saucepan or a small stockpot as a specialized piece of equipment. The choice is up to you. The breakdown by utensil gives you an idea ahead of time of what to expect: a soup, stew, pasta, stir-fry, skillet dish, roast, etc.

It is easy to shop for each meal separately; we all do in a pinch. But when you have a little extra time, it is more efficient and economical to stock up on some staples—especially non-perishable items, such as dried pasta and beans, canned tomatoes, and vegetable broth—that can be used for several recipes when you need them. Some items, such as corn tortillas, peas, chopped spinach, corn kernels, and shredded cheese, can be kept frozen and used as needed. Of course, flavorless vegetable oils like canola or safflower, as well as a bottle of good olive oil, are essential to good vegetarian cooking.

When shopping for fresh vegetables, try to choose those that are in season; they'll taste better and cost less. In addition, if you buy at farmstands and green markets, you'll be supporting your local farmer to boot. Of course, this takes a little getting used to. After all, this is a big country, and the seasons vary. To further confuse the issue, produce often travels great distances to reach us. And those of us who live in less sunny climes do not want to eat cabbage and potatoes nine months out of the year. So when it is growing season, look for the produce that is most plentiful and looks freshest, or ask your produce manager what is local. More and more supermarkets are responding to consumer demands for produce that not only looks good, but tastes good, too.

A few techniques make following these recipes a snap. First, take a few minutes to read the recipe start to finish before you begin, so that you have a basic idea of the procedure involved. This will help you determine whether the recipe indeed suits your needs and give you a chance to make sure you have all the ingredients. Are you interested in a casual supper of Cajun Bean Burgers or are you feeding a crowd and looking for something like my Grand Vegetable Aioli, a huge platter of colorful vegetables dipped in a heady garlic mayonnaise? Do you have a craving for a pasta without tomato sauce, perhaps Buckwheat and Bow Ties with Browned Onions, or are you in the mood for tomato sauce without the pasta, as in Spaghetti Squash with Marinara Sauce?

Now I hope you are ready to prepare some marvelous one-pot vegetarian dishes. Join the millions of Americans who are including more vegetables and grains and less meat in their diets and plunge into the exciting new world of vegetarian cooking. After all, your mother told you to eat your vegetables. She was right. Now it's fun to do so.

The Vegetarian Soup Pot

We tend to think of
*soup as a starter. But everyone can remember a
meal they wish had both begun and ended with a
great bowl of satisfying soup. So, when you're
doing the cooking, and a steaming bowl of homemade
soup hits the spot, there is no need to serve anything else for dinner, except perhaps a tossed salad
and some sturdy bread.*

   *The recipes in this chapter deliver the back-to-the-
womb security that only soup can provide. They
run the full gamut from hearty winter soups like Wild
Mushroom Bisque, chock-full of meaty mushrooms and steaming with goodness, to bowls of
Chilled Orange-Carrot Soup that cool off the sticki-
est summer nights.*

A soup pot, unlike a skillet, has tall sides. For most of these recipes a 3- or 4-quart pot is sufficient. Of course, once you start making soup a household staple, you may want to double or triple the recipes. Then, of course, you'll need a larger pot.

Many of the recipes in this chapter call for vegetable broth, which is available in cans at the supermarket or at health food stores. If you cook with a lot of vegetables, you can also use the scraps that are often discarded to make homemade vegetable stock. Use whatever is on hand, like onion or carrot ends, potato scrapings, celery leaves—the more the merrier. Save them in the refrigerator until you have a quart or more of vegetables. Then simply cover them with water and gently boil until flavorful, about half an hour. Strain, season with salt and pepper, and you have a fine stock to use immediately, refrigerate, or freeze.

If you choose to use homemade stock, remember that canned broth tends to be saltier, so you should salt to taste. Furthermore, for those who are not vegetarians, homemade or canned chicken broth can be substituted for vegetable broth. For those on a low-salt diet, reduced- sodium chicken broth is readily available. Some soups, like the Curried Vegetable Chowder, use a milk base rather than a broth base. Low-fat milk can always be substituted for whole milk.

Many of these soups, like Tomato Soup with Orzo and Parmesan Cheese or Spring Saffron Soup, are quick and easy to prepare, perfect for a weeknight supper. A few, like Spanish White Bean and Kale Soup, are more appropriate for a weekend meal, because they require longer simmering. So be sure to read the recipe through before you get started. I sometimes start soups in the morning, or use a Crock-Pot, so that they are ready when I return home from work. For further convenience, try doubling the recipes and eating leftovers, or freezing for later use. Twice the recipe is never twice the work, and soups often taste better when the flavors are left to marry.

So get your mouth set for a dazzling array of satisfying soups, including Summer Vegetable Soup with Pesto, Peppery Split Pea Soup with Garlicky Croutons, African Yam and Peanut Soup, and Garlic and Bread Soup.

Barley Soup with Escarole

This soup makes a hearty and nutritious winter meal. Barley is located with the dried beans in the supermarket.

Makes 4 servings

2 tablespoons olive oil
2 large leeks (white and tender green), well rinsed and sliced
Pinch of fennel seed
2 (14½-ounce) cans vegetable broth
¼ cup dry vermouth or dry white wine

3 garlic cloves, minced
¾ cup pearl barley
1 medium head of escarole, root end removed, chopped
¾ teaspoon freshly ground pepper
⅓ cup grated Parmesan cheese

1) In a small soup pot, heat the olive oil over medium heat. Add the leeks and fennel seed. Cook, stirring occasionally, until the leeks are softened and translucent, about 5 minutes.

2) Add the broth, vermouth, and 1½ cups water. Bring to a boil over high heat. Stir in the garlic and barley. Reduce the heat to medium-low, cover, and cook until the barley is tender but still springy, about 45 minutes.

3) Stir in the escarole and pepper; remove from the heat. Let stand for about 1 minute, until the escarole is wilted. Ladle into soup bowls, sprinkle the Parmesan cheese on top, and serve.

Butternut Squash Soup with Fresh Ginger

The play of the sweet and hearty squash against the spicy ginger makes this pretty soup a warming meal for a winter day. It is even better the second day.

Makes 4 servings

1 large butternut squash (about 3 pounds)
2 teaspoons vegetable oil
1 medium onion, sliced
2½ teaspoons grated fresh ginger
3 garlic cloves, minced
1 (14½-ounce) can vegetable broth

2½ cups milk
¼ teaspoon salt
⅛ teaspoon cayenne
1 teaspoon butter
Pinch of allspice
¼ cup sour cream

1) With a sharp knife, cut the stem off the squash; then cut the squash lengthwise in half. With a spoon, scoop out the seeds. Cut each half in half again to facilitate peeling. Peel the squash pieces carefully with a small sharp knife and cut them into 2-inch chunks.

2) In a medium soup pot, heat the oil over medium heat. Add the onion and cook, stirring occasionally, until it is softened and translucent, 3 to 5 minutes.

3) Add the ginger, garlic, squash, broth, milk, salt, and cayenne. Bring to a boil over high heat, then reduce the heat to medium. Cook until the squash is very soft, 10 to 15 minutes.

4) Puree the soup, in batches if necessary, in a food processor until very smooth. Pour the soup back into the pot. Add the butter and allspice. Reduce the heat to medium-low, cover, and cook for 15 minutes. Season with additional salt and cayenne to taste. Serve hot, topped with a dollop of sour cream.

Warm Cabbage Borscht

Shredding the vegetables in a *food processor makes this classic a simple soup to prepare.*

Makes 4 to 6 servings

2 tablespoons vegetable oil
1 small onion, finely chopped
1 small celery rib, finely chopped
1 (16-ounce) can stewed
  tomatoes
1 carrot, shredded
4 garlic cloves, minced
2½ cups shredded cabbage
2 medium beets, peeled and
  grated

1 (14½-ounce) can vegetable
  broth
⅛ teaspoon salt
⅛ teaspoon freshly ground
  pepper
6 tablespoons sour cream
1½ tablespoons chopped fresh
  dill

1) In a large soup pot, heat the oil over medium heat. Add the onion and celery and cook, stirring occasionally, until the onion is softened and translucent, 3 to 5 minutes.

2) Add the stewed tomatoes, carrot, and garlic. Cook, stirring occasionally, for 10 minutes.

3) Add the cabbage, beets, vegetable broth, salt, and pepper. Cook for 40 minutes, or until the cabbage is tender. Serve hot, topped with sour cream and sprinkled with dill.

Cold Gingered Cantaloupe Soup

This simple no-cook soup will *cool down any hot summer night.*

Makes 3 to 4 servings

1 cantaloupe
1 cup fresh or canned
  unsweetened pineapple
  chunks
½ cup orange juice, preferably
  fresh

¼ cup fresh lime juice
3 tablespoons shredded fresh
  ginger
1 kiwi, peeled, halved, and
  thinly sliced

1) Cut the cantaloupe in half and scoop out the seeds with a spoon. Quarter the melon halves. Cut off the rind with a sharp knife and cut each piece of melon into large chunks.

2) In a food processor, combine the melon, pineapple, orange juice, and lime juice. Puree until very smooth.

3) Place the shredded ginger in the center of a piece of cheesecloth, gather up the ends, and twist to squeeze out as much ginger juice as possible into a small bowl or measuring cup. Stir 1½ teaspoons of this juice into the soup. Cover and refrigerate until well chilled, at least 2 hours.

4) To serve, ladle the soup into 3 or 4 small bowls. Garnish each bowl with the kiwi arranged in a pinwheel design on top.

Chilled Orange-Carrot Soup

Makes 3 to 4 servings

2 tablespoons butter
1 tablespoon vegetable oil
3 medium leeks (white part only), well rinsed and chopped
1 tablespoon curry powder
1½ pounds carrots, peeled and sliced
2 (14½-ounce) cans vegetable or reduced-sodium chicken broth

1 cup orange juice, preferably fresh
¼ teaspoon grated orange zest
¼ teaspoon cayenne
¼ teaspoon salt
½ cup sour cream or plain yogurt
1 tablespoon chopped cilantro, parsley, or scallion greens

1) In a small soup pot, melt the butter in the oil over medium heat. Add the leeks and curry powder. Cook, stirring often, until the leeks are soft and translucent, 3 to 5 minutes.

2) Add the carrots and broth. Bring to a boil, reduce the heat to medium, and cook until the carrots are soft, about 15 minutes. In a food processor, puree the soup until smooth.

3) Pour the soup into a medium bowl. Stir in the orange juice, orange zest, cayenne, and salt. Cover and refrigerate until well chilled, at least 2 hours. Season with additional salt to taste. Serve topped with sour cream or yogurt and cilantro.

Dinner Gazpacho

Hard-boiled eggs, the only cooked component of this dish, thicken the gazpacho and add protein to turn this light starter into a main-course soup. Much of this easy soup is prepared in a food processor; there's no need to rinse the bowl between steps. Allow at least 2 hours for the soup to chill. ***Makes 4 servings***

2 eggs
2 garlic cloves, minced
½ medium red onion, sliced
1 green bell pepper, quartered
2 cucumbers, peeled, seeded, and finely diced
3 large tomatoes, quartered
1 quart tomato juice
Juice of 1 lime

1½ tablespoons balsamic or red wine vinegar
2 teaspoons Worcestershire sauce
1 teaspoon salt
⅛ to ¼ teaspoon Tabasco sauce, to taste
3 tablespoons olive oil
½ cup croutons
2 scallions, thinly sliced

1) Place the eggs in a small saucepan. Cover with water and bring to a boil. Reduce the heat to a simmer and cook for 10 minutes. Drain and cool down in cold water. Peel at once and set aside.

2) In a food processor, combine the garlic, red onion, bell pepper, and half of the cucumbers. Puree until smooth. Remove to a large bowl.

3) Dice 1 of the tomatoes; reserve with the remaining cucumber for garnish. Pulse the rest of the tomatoes in the food processor until chunky. Add to the puree in the bowl. Stir in the tomato juice.

4) In the food processor, combine the shelled eggs, lime juice, vinegar, Worcestershire, salt, and Tabasco. Puree until smooth. With the machine on, slowly add the olive oil. Stir thoroughly into the soup.

5) Cover and refrigerate until well chilled, at least 2 hours. Serve in soup bowls, with the croutons, scallions, cucumber, and tomatoes sprinkled on top.

Garlic and Bread Soup

Four heads of garlic? You bet! *Yet this soup is surprisingly subtle, because roasting garlic mellows its flavor considerably. For a substantial meal in a bowl, this festive soup is thickened with whole wheat bread, then topped with chopped tomatoes and large croutons dripping with melted Swiss cheese.*

Makes 4 servings

4 heads of garlic
3 tablespoons olive oil
8 slices of French bread
1 large onion, chopped
1 carrot, thinly sliced
1 celery rib, chopped
1 (14½-ounce) can diced peeled tomatoes, drained
1 (14½-ounce) can vegetable broth

¼ teaspoon dried sage
⅛ teaspoon freshly ground pepper
3 slices of soft whole wheat bread
1 cup milk
½ cup shredded Swiss cheese
3 plum tomatoes, chopped
1 tablespoon chopped parsley

1) Preheat the oven to 375 degrees F. Cut the garlic heads in half through their circumference, drizzle with 1 tablespoon olive oil, and place the halves together again. Wrap in foil and roast until soft, about 35 minutes. Remove from the oven, unwrap, and let stand until cool enough to handle, about 5 minutes.

2) While the garlic is roasting, toast the French bread slices in a single layer on a baking sheet in the oven, turning once, until very crisp (they will soften in the soup), about 15 minutes. Remove from the oven and set aside. (Leave the oven on to melt the cheese later.)

3) In a medium soup pot, heat the remaining 2 tablespoons oil over medium heat. Add the onion, carrot, and celery. Cook, stirring occasionally, until the onion is softened and translucent, about 5 minutes.

4) Add the canned tomatoes, broth, sage, pepper, and 1¾ cups water. Bring to a boil, reduce the heat to medium, and cook for 5 minutes.

5) Squeeze the roasted garlic from the skins into the bowl of a food processor. Blend with the whole wheat bread and milk until smooth. Stir into the the soup and cook, stirring occasionally, until heated through, 3 to 5 minutes. While the soup is heating, sprinkle the cheese over the French bread and return to the oven until the cheese is melted, about 5 minutes.

6) To serve, divide the chopped plum tomatoes among the bowls. Ladle the hot soup over them. Top with the Swiss cheese croutons, garnish with the parsley, and serve immediately.

Curried Lentil Soup with Greens

This is a fine recipe to double *or triple, as leftovers freeze well and the soup can also be tossed with pasta to act as a sauce. Reduce the water to 4½ cups, and this becomes a fine stew.*

Makes 4 to 6 servings

2 tablespoons olive oil
1 medium onion, chopped
1½ tablespoons curry powder
2 garlic cloves, minced
1 cup lentils, rinsed and picked
   over

1 (14½-ounce) can stewed
   tomatoes
1 cup chopped greens (kale,
   Swiss chard, or spinach)
½ teaspoon salt
½ cup plain yogurt or sour cream

1) In a small soup pot, heat the oil over medium heat. Add the onion and curry and cook, stirring often, until the onion starts to brown, 7 to 10 minutes.

2) Add the garlic, lentils, and 6 cups of water. Bring to a boil, reduce the heat to medium, and cook over medium heat until the lentils are tender, 40 to 45 minutes.

3) Stir in the tomatoes, greens, and salt. Cook until the greens are wilted but still bright green, 2 to 3 minutes. Serve topped with a dollop of yogurt or sour cream.

Wild Mushroom Bisque

Chock-full of three kinds of mushrooms, this luxurious soup is a mushroom lover's dream come true. Dried shiitakes are usually stocked in the Asian section of your supermarket. And for convenience, sliced mushrooms can be purchased in many supermarkets.   **Makes 4 servings**

4 medium dried shiitake
  mushrooms
1 tablespoon butter
1 tablespoon olive oil
½ teaspoon dried thyme leaves
½ cup finely chopped shallots
½ pound fresh shiitake or other
  wild mushrooms, stemmed,
  caps sliced

½ pound white button
  mushrooms, sliced
½ teaspoon salt
⅛ teaspoon freshly ground pepper
3 tablespoons flour
3¼ cups hot milk
2 tablespoons medium-dry
  sherry
2 tablespoons chopped parsley

1) In a small bowl, soak the dried mushrooms in ⅓ cup hot tap water until softened, about 15 minutes. Remove the mushrooms and squeeze as much liquid as possible back into the bowl. Cut off and discard the stems; finely chop the caps. Strain and reserve the soaking water.

2) In a medium soup pot, melt the butter in the oil over medium heat. Add the thyme and shallots. Cook, stirring frequently, until the shallots are very lightly browned, about 5 minutes. Add the chopped mushrooms, fresh shiitakes, white mushrooms, salt, and pepper to the pot. Cook, stirring gently, until the shiitakes are tender, 5 to 8 minutes.

3) Sprinkle the flour evenly over the mushrooms. Reduce the heat to medium-low and cook, stirring with a wooden spoon or spatula and continuously scraping the bottom of the pot to avoid sticking, for 2 minutes.

4) Gradually whisk in the hot milk. Bring to a boil over high heat, stirring until the soup thickens slightly. Pour in the reserved shiitake soaking liquid and the sherry. Reduce the heat and simmer for 2 to 3 minutes. Add the parsley and season with additional salt and pepper to taste. Serve hot.

Peppery Split Pea Soup with Garlicky Croutons

A creamy texture, aromatic green peppercorns, and healthy homemade croutons make this effortless low-fat soup distinctive. Green peppercorns can be found packed in brine in jars near the olives and capers in the supermarket.

Makes 6 to 8 servings

2 teaspoons green peppercorns in brine, well drained
2 tablespoons olive oil
1 medium onion, chopped
2 medium carrots, peeled and thinly sliced
2 celery ribs, thinly sliced

1 pound split peas (about 2 cups)
4 garlic cloves, peeled and cut in half
1 teaspoon salt
½ teaspoon freshly ground pepper
6 slices of whole wheat bread
½ cup sour cream or plain yogurt

1) On a small cutting board, crush the green peppercorns with the back of a teaspoon. With a kitchen knife, scrape the peppercorns and their juices into a medium soup pot. Add the oil, onion, carrots, and celery. Cook over medium heat, stirring occasionally, until the onion just starts to brown, 5 to 7 minutes.

2) Add the split peas, 10 cups of water, 1 garlic clove, the salt, and the pepper. Bring to a boil. Reduce the heat to medium, cover, and cook until the peas are tender, about 45 minutes; reduce the heat slightly if the soup starts to boil over.

3) Meanwhile, toast the bread until very crisp, then rub the warm toast with the remaining cut garlic cloves. Remove the crusts and cut the toast into large cubes.

4) When the peas are soft, puree the soup in batches in a food processor until smooth. Return to the soup pot and heat through. To serve, ladle the soup into bowls, sprinkle a generous portion of the croutons on top, and spoon a dollop of sour cream into the center of each bowl.

Italian Roasted Red Pepper and Tomato Soup

For this dish, use sun-dried *tomatoes that are not packed in oil. In fact, this soup has no added fat at all, yet it is packed with flavor.* **Makes 6 to 8 servings**

5 dry-pack sun-dried tomato halves
2 large red bell peppers
3 large tomatoes or 1 (14½-ounce) can peeled plum tomatoes, drained and seeded
2 garlic cloves, minced

2 cups Vegetable Stock (recipe follows) or water
⅓ cup chopped fresh basil
1 tablespoon balsamic vinegar
Pinch of cayenne
3 tablespoons grated Parmesan cheese

1) In a small bowl, cover the sun-dried tomatoes with hot tap water and let stand until soft, about 15 minutes. Drain and reserve.

2) Roast the peppers by setting them directly over a gas flame or under a broiler, turning frequently, until they are black, 7 to 10 minutes. Place in a bag and let stand until cool enough to handle, discard the stems, seeds, and ribs; remove the skin with your hands or scrape it off firmly with a knife. Don't worry if there are black flakes left on the peppers.

3) If you are using fresh tomatoes, roast them by setting them on the gas flame or under a broiler and rotating them with tongs until their skins start to peel, 3 to 5 minutes. When they are cool enough to handle, peel them, halve them, and remove the seeds. If you are using canned tomatoes, skip this step.

4) In a food processor, combine the sun-dried tomatoes, roasted peppers, fresh or canned tomatoes, garlic, and ¼ cup of the broth. Puree until smooth. Pour into a soup pot.

5) Add the remaining broth, half the basil, the balsamic vinegar, and cayenne. Bring to a boil; reduce the heat to medium-low, cover, and simmer for 10 minutes. Stir in the remaining basil. Ladle the soup into warm bowls, sprinkle the Parmesan cheese on top, and serve.

Vegetable Stock

If you cook with fresh *vegetables, it is easy to make vegetable stock with leftovers and/or household staples. Don't use peels unless they are organic, but otherwise most clean vegetable scraps will do. The few exceptions to this rule are eggplant, strong greens (with the exception of kale), and vegetables in the cabbage family, like turnips and broccoli. Otherwise, experiment with any vegetables on hand. Onions, carrots, and celery always make a good base for vegetable stock, but seasonal items like corncobs, ripe tomatoes, and fresh herbs add extra dimension. A pinch of crushed hot red peppers, added to the stock 10 minutes before it is strained, balances the natural sweetness of the vegetables with a little spiciness. Season later with salt to taste. This recipe can be doubled easily.* ***Makes 3 to 4 cups***

4 cups cold water
3½ cups sliced vegetables, at
    least 3 kinds, such as onions,
    carrots, and celery
6 garlic cloves, crushed with the
    side of a knife

5 sprigs of parsley
Pinch of dried thyme
1 bay leaf

Simmer all the ingredients together, uncovered, until the vegetables have no flavor left in them, about 45 minutes. Strain, pressing down on the vegetables to extract their juices.

Quinoa Soup with Corn

This summery low-fat soup cooks in fifteen minutes, and it is tasty hot or cold. Quinoa (keen-wa) is an ancient grain that is extremely high in protein. It was a staple in the Incan diet and is still eaten by South American Indians. You can find it in many supermarkets near the rice and in all health food stores. **Makes 4 servings**

1 (14½-ounce) can vegetable broth
½ cup quinoa, rinsed
2 garlic cloves, minced
¼ teaspoon cayenne
1 cup fresh or frozen corn kernels
1½ tablespoons chopped cilantro or parsley
1 tablespoon fresh lime juice

1) In a small soup pot, combine the broth, quinoa, garlic, cayenne, and 1¾ cups water. Bring to a boil, reduce the heat to medium, and cook 10 minutes.

2) Add the corn kernels and cook until hot and tender, about 3 minutes. Stir in the cilantro and cook 1 minute. Remove from the heat and stir in the lime juice. Serve hot or cold.

Ricotta Wonton Ravioli Soup

East meets West when
Chinese wonton skins are filled with Italian ricotta and
Parmesan cheese. These hybrid wonton ravioli are a snap to
assemble and light as a cloud. Wonton wrappers can be found
in the produce section of most supermarkets. ***Makes 4 servings***

½ cup ricotta
2 tablespoons grated Parmesan
    cheese
1½ tablespoons minced parsley
Pinch of salt
Pinch of freshly ground pepper

20 wonton skins
2 (14½-ounce) cans vegetable
    broth
2 medium carrots
¼ pound snow peas, cut
    lengthwise into thin strips

1) In a small bowl, combine the ricotta, Parmesan cheese, parsley, salt,
and pepper.

2) To prevent drying, work in batches. Lay 4 wonton skins on the
counter. Place a scant teaspoon of the ricotta mixture in the middle of
each wonton. Using a small bowl of water, wet your fingers lightly and brush
them along 2 sides of the wonton skins. Fold the skins in half point to
point to form a triangle. Press the ends down firmly, gently pushing in toward
the filling until well sealed. Repeat with the remaining wontons and
filling. Cover the filled wontons with plastic if they start to dry out.

3) In a medium soup pot, bring the broth to a boil, then reduce the heat
to medium or lower so the broth is just simmering. Using a vegetable
peeler, discard the carrot peel, and then peel long strips of the carrots right
into the soup until you can peel no longer. Carefully add the wontons
and snow peas to the broth, stirring gently to prevent sticking. Cook until the
wontons are tender, 2 to 3 minutes. Serve immediately in warm bowls.

Spring Saffron Soup

If you reserve a few sprigs of *the frilly fennel top, they make a lovely garnish. Saffron, the most luxurious of all spices, can be found at all specialty food shops.*

Makes 4 to 6 servings

1 fennel bulb
1½ tablespoons olive oil
3 leeks (white and tender green),
   well rinsed and chopped
4 garlic cloves, chopped
2 (14½-ounce) cans vegetable
   broth

4 medium red potatoes, peeled
   and cut into ½-inch dice
1⅓ cups fresh or frozen peas
⅛ teaspoon saffron threads
⅛ teaspoon cayenne
¼ cup dry vermouth or dry
   white wine

1) If the green fronds are still attached to the fennel bulb, chop 1 to 2 tablespoons and set aside. Remove the outer stalks from the fennel bulb and discard. Trim the fennel; chop the bulb. In a medium soup pot, heat the oil over medium heat. Add the leeks, fennel, and garlic. Cook, stirring occasionally, until the leeks are wilted but not browned, about 5 minutes.

2) Add the broth and 1¾ cups water. Bring the liquid to a boil. Add the potatoes. Reduce the heat to medium, cover, and cook until the potatoes are tender, 15 to 20 minutes.

3) Add the peas, saffron, cayenne, and vermouth. Cook until the peas are tender and warmed through, 2 to 5 minutes, depending on whether the peas are frozen or fresh.

Tomato Soup with Orzo and Parmesan Cheese

The combination of orzo, the *tiny rice-shaped pasta, and freshly grated Parmesan cheese, turns this quick and flavorful soup into a satisfying dinner. Serve with bread and a tossed salad on the side.* ***Makes 4 servings***

2 tablespoons olive oil
1 large onion, chopped
1 small green bell pepper, chopped
2 garlic cloves, chopped
½ teaspoon dried oregano
⅓ cup orzo
1 (28-ounce) can crushed tomatoes

1 (14½-ounce) can vegetable broth
⅛ teaspoon salt
⅛ teaspoon freshly ground pepper
¼ cup grated Parmesan cheese

1) In a medium soup pot, heat the oil over medium heat. Add the onion, green bell pepper, garlic, and oregano. Cook, stirring occasionally, until the onions are softened and translucent, 3 to 5 minutes.

2) Add the orzo, crushed tomatoes, vegetable broth, salt, and pepper. Bring to a boil, reduce the heat to medium, and cook until the orzo is tender but still firm, 7 to 9 minutes.

3) Stir 3 tablespoons of the Parmesan cheese into the soup. Ladle into warm bowls and sprinkle the remaining cheese on top.

Curried Vegetable Chowder

This hearty, colorful, low-fat chowder is distinguished by the contrasting flavors of tangy broccoli rabe and sweet carrots. ***Makes 4 servings***

2 tablespoons vegetable oil
3 medium leeks (white and
   tender green), well rinsed
   and chopped
3 tablespoons flour
1 tablespoon plus ½ teaspoon
   curry powder
4 medium carrots, peeled, cut
   lengthwise in half, then sliced
   crosswise 1 inch thick

1 medium red potato, cut into
   ½-inch cubes
2¾ cups milk
¾ teaspoon salt
1 small bunch of broccoli rabe,
   tough ends removed, cut
   crosswise into 1-inch pieces

1) In a medium soup pot, preferably nonstick, heat the oil over medium heat. Add the leeks and cook, stirring occasionally, until they are softened and translucent but not brown, 3 to 5 minutes.

2) Reduce the heat to medium-low. Sprinkle the flour and curry powder over the leeks and cook, stirring constantly, for 2 minutes to prevent burning. (The leeks will start to brown.) Add the carrots and potato.

3) Gradually stir in the milk, scraping up any browned bits from the bottom of the pan. Bring to a boil over medium-high heat and cook until the soup coats the back of a spoon, 2 to 3 minutes.

4) Reduce the heat to medium. Add the salt and broccoli rabe. Cover and cook until the potato is soft and the carrots are tender, 5 to 10 minutes. Serve hot.

Summer Vegetable Soup with Pesto

Store-bought pesto works its magic on summer vegetables. The result is a quick and satisfying after-work supper, terrific with plenty of hearty bread. Fresh pesto is usually located next to the refrigerated fresh pasta in the supermarket. Leftover pesto freezes well.

Makes 4 servings

1 (14½-ounce) can vegetable broth
1 medium red potato, peeled and cut into ½-inch dice
1 large plum tomato, diced
¼ pound green beans, trimmed and cut into thirds

1 small summer squash, cut into ½-inch dice
1 ear of corn or ¾ cup frozen corn kernels
⅓ cup pesto

1) In a medium soup pot, combine the broth, potatoes, tomatoes, and 1¾ cups water. Bring to a boil and cook until the potatoes are about half done, about 5 minutes.

2) Reduce the heat to medium, add the green beans, and continue to cook for another 2 minutes. Add the summer squash and corn and cook for 3 minutes, or until both the beans and potatoes are tender.

3) Turn off the heat. In a small bowl, stir the pesto well. Mix in ⅓ cup of hot broth from the soup. Stir the hot pesto into the soup. Serve immediately.

Spanish White Bean and Kale Soup

Don't be misled by the bountiful amount of garlic in this beautiful peasant soup. It mellows with long cooking. If you want to freeze the soup, do so before the kale is added. Since the beans are best if soaked overnight, be sure to plan a day ahead. **Makes 6 to 8 servings**

2 cups dried white beans
3 tablespoons olive oil
2 medium onions, chopped
1½ teaspoons dried marjoram
16 garlic cloves, peeled and
  sliced
1 (14½-ounce) can diced peeled
  tomatoes, drained

3 cups shredded kale leaves
2 teaspoons red wine vinegar
2 teaspoons salt
¾ teaspoon freshly ground
  pepper

1) In a large soup pot, cover the beans with at least 2 inches of water. Soak 8 to 24 hours; drain.

2) In the soup pot, heat the oil over medium heat. Add the onions and marjoram and cook, stirring occasionally, until the onions are soft, about 5 minutes. Add the garlic and cook until fragrant, 1 to 2 minutes.

3) Add the beans and 6 cups water. Bring to a boil, then reduce the heat to medium, and cook, covered, until the beans are tender, about 1 hour.

4) Stir the tomatoes and kale into the pot. Cook until the kale is wilted but still bright green, 2 to 4 minutes. Add the vinegar, 1 cup water, and the salt and pepper. Serve hot.

Wild Rice and Watercress Soup

Lightly browned shallots add *flavor to this elegant soup. It is perfect for a light lunch. Feel free to opt for two percent, or even skim milk, by the way.*

Makes 3 servings

⅓ cup wild rice or wild rice mix
2 tablespoons butter
½ cup chopped shallots
¼ teaspoon dried thyme leaves
3 tablespoons flour
2 cups milk
⅔ cup vegetable broth

1 tablespoon dry sherry
½ teaspoon salt
½ teaspoon freshly ground
  pepper
1 bunch of watercress, tough
  stems removed, coarsely
  chopped (about 2 cups)

1) Bring a medium soup pot of lightly salted water to a full boil. Add the wild rice and boil until the rice starts to open up, about 45 minutes. Strain and set the wild rice aside.

2) In the same pot, melt the butter over medium heat. Add the shallots and thyme and cook, stirring frequently, until the shallots just start to brown, about 3 minutes. Add the flour and cook, stirring constantly, for 2 minutes.

3) Gradually whisk in the milk and then the broth. Raise the heat to medium-high and bring to a boil, whisking until the soup is smooth and thickened, about 3 minutes.

4) Add the wild rice, sherry, salt, and pepper. Reduce the heat and simmer 3 minutes. Stir in the watercress, remove from the heat, and serve.

African Yam and Peanut Soup

This soup is even better after *several hours or the next day. The amount of salt added will depend on the saltiness of the peanut butter used.*

Makes 4 servings

3 yams (1¼ pounds), peeled and thickly sliced
1 medium onion, sliced
1 (14½-ounce) can vegetable broth

¼ teaspoon salt
¼ teaspoon cayenne
¼ cup smooth peanut butter
2 tablespoons chopped cilantro or parsley

1) In a medium soup pot or large saucepan, combine the yams, onion, broth, salt, cayenne, and 1¾ cups water. Bring to a boil, reduce the heat to medium, cover, and cook until the yams are very soft when pierced with a fork, 10 to 15 minutes.

2) With a slotted spoon, remove the yams and onions to a food processor. Puree in batches until smooth, adding extra liquid as necessary from the soup pot.

3) Whisk the peanut butter into the remaining stock in the pot. Using a rubber spatula, scrape the yam puree back into the soup pot. Reheat, stirring to mix well. Season with additional salt and cayenne to taste. Garnish with the cilantro.

Potato and Leek Soup

*T**his quickly prepared soup is a winter classic. Just make sure you use russet baking potatoes and rinse the leeks well after you slice them, so there is no trace of grit.*   ***Makes 6 servings***

6 leeks (white and tender green),
   thinly sliced and rinsed
3 medium baking potatoes,
   peeled and sliced

1 teaspoon salt
½ teaspoon freshly ground
   pepper
2½ tablespoons butter

1) In a medium soup pot, bring 2¼ cups water to a boil. Add the leeks, potatoes, and salt. Reduce the heat to medium, cover, and cook until the potatoes are soft and falling apart, about 25 minutes.

2) Add the pepper. Season with additional salt to taste. Ladle into bowls, add a pat of butter to each bowl, and serve while hot.

Vegetarian Skillet Dishes

N*o cooking is more natural and straightforward for Americans than a skillet supper. What you see is what you get. This lack of mystery turns cooking into a pleasure. Turn up the heat and you can see, hear, and smell your corn cakes cook. They smell great. Now just sneak a peak, turning them when they are golden brown. And when they're brown on the second side, flip them onto a nearby plate and gobble them up. Direct enough?*

A skillet is any wide short-sided pan, sometimes called a sauté or frying pan. There are many varieties of skillets. Most often, I reach for a cast-iron or nonstick skillet. A cast-iron skillet is indestructible and responds quickly to any change in heat. A

nonstick skillet obviously prevents sticking, allows for quick cleanup, and requires less fat. But for the following recipes, unless specified, any skillet will do.

A few simple techniques help facilitate all skillet cooking. When you want food to crisp and brown, like potato and parsnip fritters, keep them a little separated in the pan to prevent them from steaming. On the other hand, if you want food to steam, like the eggs inside the Hominy Grits 'n Eggs, cover the skillet. If a cover didn't come with the skillet or has long since disappeared, look for any pot cover that fits. In a pinch, foil will do nicely.

Also, because most skillet cooking is fairly quick, keep the ingredients by the side of the stove for easy access. This means preparing all your vegetables before you set skillet to stove. That way, once you start, it will be smooth sailing.

A flat skillet on direct heat serves as a griddle for pieces of food that need turning: pancakes, fritters, savory cakes, or vegetable burgers. Try the Zucchini Feta Fritters with yogurt. They're crisp on the outside, soft and cheesy inside. And for burger freaks, there are plenty of recipes in this chapter that may be eaten like burgers, such as the Cajun Bean Burgers, Cashew Croquettes with Tsaziki Sauce, or Tempeh Burgers with Satay Sauce.

International egg dishes make satisfying skillet suppers—Mexican Eggs in Fresh Tomato Salsa, Asparagus and Red Onion Frittata, and the quick Chinese Scrambled Eggs, to name a few. A hot skillet is also the perfect place to cook the fruits or vegetables that go into a warm salad or even fill a sandwich or tortilla, as in Fresh Mango Chutney and Brie Tortillas, Escarole Salad with Warm Pears, Blue Cheese, and Walnuts. For the best picnic food I know, try the Seared Eggplant Sandwiches with Sesame Mayonnaise.

Asparagus and Red Onion Frittata

This Italian open-faced *omelet is equally good served warm or at room temperature. It may be served with the Fresh Tomato Salsa on page 41 or the Tomato-Dill Relish on page 176.* ***Makes 4 to 6 servings***

1 pound asparagus
6 eggs
¼ cup grated Romano cheese
2 tablespoons minced red onion
¼ teaspoon salt

¼ teaspoon freshly ground
  pepper
1 tablespoon butter
1 tablespoon olive oil

1) Bring a large nonstick ovenproof skillet half filled with water to a full boil. Slice the tough bottom ends off the asparagus stalks and discard. Cook the asparagus until still bright green but slightly tender, about 5 minutes. Drain into a colander and run cold water over the asparagus. Slice the stalks into ½-inch sections.

2) In a medium bowl, whisk together the eggs, cheese, red onion, salt, and pepper. Stir in the asparagus.

3) Preheat the broiler, setting the rack at a maximum distance from the heat. In the same large skillet, melt the butter in the olive oil over low heat. Pour in the egg and asparagus mixture. Cook until the frittata is set around the edges but still runny on top, 10 to 15 minutes. Lift the edge of the frittata with a rubber spatula, tipping it to allow some of the uncooked egg to run underneath.

4) Transfer the skillet to the broiler and broil until the top just sets, 30 seconds to 1 minute. Loosen the frittata gently with a spatula and slide onto a large serving plate. Cut into wedges to serve.

Bean and Avocado Quesadillas

Even kids go berserk for these; they are the ultimate healthy grilled cheese sandwiches. Look for ripe avocados with bumpy skins to deliver the flavor needed for this dish. If you have one, a cast-iron skillet works very well for quesadillas. **Makes 4 servings (8 quesadillas)**

1 ripe avocado, halved, with skin and pit removed
1 tablespoon fresh lime juice
1 (14½-ounce) can black or red beans, rinsed and drained
¼ cup salsa
2½ tablespoons chopped cilantro

1 jalapeño pepper, seeded and minced
½ teaspoon salt
16 (7-inch) flour tortillas
1¼ cups shredded Monterey jack cheese
1½ tablespoons vegetable oil
4 lime wedges

1) In a medium bowl, mash the avocado and lime juice together with a fork or potato masher. Shake the beans dry, add them to the avocado, and continue to mash until the beans are still chunky but well combined. Stir in the salsa, cilantro, jalapeño pepper, and salt.

2) Preheat the oven to 200 degrees F. Lay 1 tortilla on the counter and spread about 2½ tablespoons of filling all over it, leaving a 1-inch border. Sprinkle about 2½ tablespoons of cheese on top of the filling. Lay a second tortilla on top and press all the way around. (Don't worry if they don't adhere well; the melted cheese will hold them together well enough.) Repeat with the remaining tortillas and filling.

3) Brush a large skillet with half of the vegetable oil and turn the heat to medium-high. Add the quesadillas to the hot skillet one at a time, adding a little more oil if they begin to stick. Cook for 1 minute on the first side, then turn and cook the second side until the cheese is totally melted, 1 to 2 minutes. (You can sneak a peak until you get the hang of it.) Remove to a platter in the oven until they are all cooked. When ready to serve, cut each quesadilla into 4 wedges. Accompany with lime wedges to squeeze on top.

Cajun Bean Burgers

These burgers are terrific on hard rolls with any classic burger toppings or even homemade (page 41) or store-bought salsa.

Makes 4 servings

1 (19-ounce) can kidney beans, rinsed and drained well
1 small onion, chopped
1 tablespoon grainy mustard
1 tablespoon ketchup
2 teaspoons Worcestershire sauce
¼ teaspoon cayenne
¼ teaspoon freshly ground black pepper
¼ teaspoon dried oregano,
¼ teaspoon dried thyme leaves
Pinch of black pepper
½ teaspoon salt
1 egg, lightly beaten
3 tablespoons flour
1 tablespoon vegetable oil

1) In a medium bowl, using a potato masher or fork, mash the beans, leaving them chunky. Add all the remaining ingredients except the oil and mix well.

2) In a large skillet, heat the oil over medium-high heat. With a large serving spoon, place one-fourth of the bean mixture in the pan, spreading it out with the spoon to form a round about ½ inch thick. Repeat with the remaining 3 burgers.

3) Turn the burgers when they are well browned on the bottom, about 4 minutes. Reduce the heat to medium and cook about 4 minutes longer, until cooled through and browned on the second side. Serve as you would any burgers.

Corn Cakes with Sun-Dried Tomato Sauce

Makes 4 servings

6 sun-dried tomato halves
1½ tablespoons olive oil
¼ cup chopped shallots
1¼ cups chopped plum tomatoes
½ teaspoon salt
Pinch of crushed hot red pepper
16 ounces cottage cheese
⅓ cup cornmeal, preferably
   stone-ground

⅓ cup milk
3 eggs
1 medium zucchini, shredded
1 cup fresh or frozen corn
   kernels
2 tablespoons chopped fresh dill
   or parsley
Pinch of cayenne
Dill sprigs, for garnish

1) In a small bowl, cover the sun-dried tomatoes with hot tap water and let stand until they start to soften, about 15 minutes. Drain, chop, and set aside.

2) In a large nonstick skillet, heat the olive oil over medium heat. Add half the shallots and cook, stirring frequently, until translucent, about 3 minutes. Add the sun-dried tomatoes, plum tomatoes, ¼ teaspoon salt, crushed hot red pepper, and 2 tablespoons water. Cook for 15 minutes, stirring occasionally, to marry the flavors. Scrape into a microwave-safe bowl. Rinse and dry the skillet.

3) In a medium bowl, thoroughly mix the cottage cheese, cornmeal, milk, and eggs. Add the shredded zucchini, corn, chopped dill, remaining ¼ teaspoon salt, cayenne, and remaining shallots.

4) Spray the skillet with vegetable spray, then heat the pan over medium heat. Drop the batter by heaping tablespoons into the pan, spreading it a bit with the back of the spoon. Cook the cakes in batches, turning, until they are lightly browned on both sides, about 2 minutes per side. The cakes can be served as they are cooked, with the reheated sauce spooned onto them, or held in a 200 degree F oven, until they are all ready to be served. Garnish with a sprig of dill.

Cashew Croquettes with Tsaziki Sauce

Surprisingly, *instant oatmeal is the secret ingredient in these subtle, crunchy vegetarian burgers. Tsaziki, a Greek staple made with yogurt and cucumber, makes a tangy sauce. Kirby cucumbers are the small pickling cucumbers. The cashews may be chopped by pulsing them a few times in the food processor.* **Makes 4 servings**

1 cup plain yogurt
1 kirby or ½ small cucumber, halved lengthwise, seeded, and shredded
1 garlic clove, minced
1 teaspoon chopped fresh mint or ¼ teaspoon dried
¼ teaspoon salt
⅜ teaspoon freshly ground pepper

4 (1-ounce) envelopes plain instant oatmeal
⅓ cup chopped dry-roasted cashews
1 egg, lightly beaten
1 small onion, chopped
2½ tablespoons olive oil
1 small head of lettuce

1) Place a coffee filter in a sieve over a small bowl. Pour the yogurt into the filter and let drain for 20 to 30 minutes to thicken a bit. Transfer to a medium bowl.

2) In the sink, using your hands, squeeze the excess water out of the cucumber. Add the cucumber to the yogurt. Stir in the garlic, mint, salt, and pepper. Set the tsaziki aside.

3) In a medium bowl, mix 3 envelopes of the oatmeal with ½ cup hot water. Let stand for 5 minutes. Add the cashews, egg, and onion. Mix well.

4) Evenly spread the contents of the remaining oatmeal package onto a plate. Spoon one-fourth of the cashew mixture onto the plate and press down into the oatmeal, forming a croquette no thicker than ½ inch. Turn the croquette over and press oatmeal into the other side. Repeat with the remaining croquettes.

5) In a large nonstick skillet, heat the olive oil over medium-high heat. When the oil is hot, place the croquettes in the pan. Cook, turning, until they are well browned, about 3 minutes on each side. Serve on a bed of lettuce, accompanied by the tsaziki sauce.

Chinese Scrambled Eggs

T*he addition of healthy, flavorful vegetables turns a simple scrambled egg supper into a satisfying one-pot meal. Accompany the eggs with plain toasted bagels or crusty French bread. Canned bamboo shoots are found in the Asian section of most supermarkets.*

Makes 3 to 4 servings

6 eggs
2 large scallions, sliced, white
   and green separated
2 tablespoons chopped cilantro
½ teaspoon salt
¼ cup chopped bamboo shoots
2 tablespoons vegetable oil

2 slices of fresh ginger
5 medium mushrooms, sliced
½ cup fresh bean sprouts, well
   drained
¼ to ½ teaspoon hot chili oil, to
   taste

1) In a medium bowl, whisk together the eggs, scallion greens, cilantro, salt, and 1 tablespoon water. Add the bamboo shoots and set the bowl by the side of the stove.

2) In a large nonstick skillet, heat the oil over medium heat. Add the scallion whites, ginger, mushrooms, and bean sprouts. Cook, stirring frequently, until the mushrooms are wilted and aromatic, about 3 minutes. Remove and discard the ginger.

3) Whisk the eggs again and pour over the vegetables. Reduce the heat to medium-low and cook, stirring constantly with a spatula, until the eggs are set but still soft and not rubbery, about 3 minutes. Stir in the hot chili oil and serve immediately.

Mexican Eggs in Fresh Tomato Salsa

For a quick taste of Mexico, this dish can't be beat. It is also a great way to cook eggs effortlessly, with no extra fat. Serve for brunch or dinner, with bread or warm tortillas. **Makes 4 servings**

10 plum tomatoes, quartered
¼ cup finely chopped onion
2 or 3 jalapeño peppers, to taste,
   seeded and minced

⅓ cup chopped cilantro
½ teaspoon salt
6 eggs

1) In a food processor, pulse the tomatoes until coarsely chopped. Add the tomatoes, onion, jalapeño peppers, cilantro, and salt to a large skillet with a lid. Bring to a simmer over high heat.

2) Reduce the heat to medium. With a tablespoon, make a slight indentation for each egg halfway down into the salsa. Crack the eggs into the indentations, cover the skillet, and cook for 10 minutes.

3) Uncover and tip the skillet to one side. Spoon the hot liquid over the tops of the egg whites to help cook them through. Cover and cook, until the egg whites are just cooked through but the yolks are still soft, about 10 minutes longer. Bring the skillet to the table and serve immediately with a large spoon.

Seared Eggplant Sandwiches with Sesame Mayonnaise

These elegant sandwiches make fabulous picnic fare. Just remember to allow time for the eggplant to sit for at least half an hour before cooking.

Makes 4 to 6 servings

1 large eggplant, cut crosswise into ½-inch rounds
¾ teaspoon salt
¼ cup vegetable oil
⅛ teaspoon aniseed
2 tablespoons soy sauce
1 minced garlic clove
1 tablespoon sugar
1 tablespoon rice vinegar
1 teaspoon Asian sesame oil
⅓ cup mayonnaise
2 baguettes of French bread
4 scallions, chopped
1 large bunch of watercress, tough stems removed

1) Lay the eggplant on a baking sheet in a single layer. Sprinkle with half the salt and turn the slices over. Sprinkle the second side with the remaining salt. Let stand for 30 minutes to 1 hour to let the juices exude. Pat dry with paper towels.

2) When the eggplant is ready, brush a large nonstick skillet with a thin layer of vegetable oil and set over medium-high heat. Add the eggplant in batches and cook, brushing additional oil onto the pan as needed, until the eggplant is lightly browned outside and soft all the way through, about 4 minutes on each side. Set the eggplant aside on the baking sheet or a plate as it cooks.

3) Add the aniseed, soy sauce, garlic, sugar, and vinegar to the skillet. Cover over medium heat, stirring continuously, until the liquid is reduced to half, 1 to 2 minutes. Remove from the heat and stir in the sesame oil and mayonnaise. Whisk until thoroughly combined.

4) To assemble the sandwiches: Split both baguettes horizontally in half. Remove a little bread from the center of the 2 top halves. With a knife, evenly apply about one-fourth of the mayonnaise to each of the halves.

(It is quite potent, so a little goes a long way.) Lay half the cooked eggplant along each of the bottom baguette halves. Sprinkle the scallions and watercress over the eggplant. Place the top baguette halves over the watercress and press down firmly. When ready to serve, slice the sandwiches into thirds or quarters.

Cottage Cheese Pancakes with Blueberry Sauce

For a quick brunch or a *breakfast-as-dinner, this meal can't be beat. Like all pancakes, they are best right out of the skillet, but they hold well for a short time on a platter in a 200 degree F oven. My mom likes to serve these with a side dish of melon cubes dressed with a squeeze of fresh lime juice and a sprinkling of chopped mint leaves.*

Makes 4 to 6 servings

2 cups fresh or frozen
  blueberries
1½ teaspoons cornstarch
¼ cup maple syrup
1½ cups cottage cheese

1½ cups Bisquick or other
  pancake mix
3 eggs
1 cup milk
1 tablespoon sugar

1) In a large nonstick skillet, cook the blueberries with 1 tablespoon water over medium-high heat until they are warm, 2 to 5 minutes. In a small bowl, blend the cornstarch with the maple syrup; add to the blueberries. Bring to a boil, stirring to thicken, about 1 minute. Pour the sauce into a microwavable pitcher. Stir in 3 more tablespoons water. Rinse and dry the skillet.

2) In a medium bowl, combine the cottage cheese, Bisquick, eggs, milk, and sugar. Coat the skillet generously with cooking spray. Over medium-high heat, drop tablespoons of the batter into the hot pan. Cook the pancakes in batches until they are lightly browned underneath and can easily be turned, about 2 minutes. Flip and cook on the other side until lightly browned as well, about 1 minute.

3) Remove the pancakes to plates. Top with the blueberry sauce, which can be reheated in the microwave, if necessary. Serve immediately.

Escarole Salad with Warm Pears, Blue Cheese, and Walnuts

Melted cheese, warm sweet pear slices, earthy nuts, and slightly bitter greens are combined to make this salad of contrasts. Use any kind of pear that is ripe but still a bit firm. This recipe is effortless if all the ingredients are ready by the side of the stove before you begin.

Makes 3 to 4 servings

1 medium head of escarole
1 tablespoon red wine vinegar
¼ teaspoon salt
¼ teaspoon freshly ground pepper

⅓ cup crumbled Gorgonzola, Roquefort, or blue cheese
1 large pear
3 tablespoons vegetable oil
½ cup chopped walnuts

1) Rinse and dry the escarole leaves, then tear them into 3 or 4 pieces each. Place in a large bowl by the side of the stove next to the vinegar, salt, pepper, and cheese.

2) Cut the pear in half lengthwise. Remove the stem and scoop out the seeds with a spoon. Cut into ½-inch slices.

3) In a large skillet, heat the oil over medium-high heat. Add the pears and nuts. Cook, constantly stirring the nuts and turning the pears, until the pears are warmed through but not mushy, 3 to 5 minutes.

4) Turn off the heat and stir in the vinegar. Immediately pour the pears and walnuts over the escarole, using a rubber spatula or wooden spoon to scrape all the dressing out of the skillet. Sprinkle the salt, pepper, and cheese evenly over the top of the salad. Toss gently. Serve immediately with tongs or serving spoons.

Falafel Salad with Tahini Dressing

Falafel mix turns this Middle Eastern standby into an instant dinner. Tahini, Middle Eastern sesame paste, may be found with the specialty food items in most supermarkets. Stir it well before you use it, because the oil tends to separate out. The lettuce may either be left in whole leaves or torn into large bite-size pieces. **Makes 4 servings**

1 (6-ounce) box falafel mix
1 small head of green leaf or
  romaine lettuce
⅓ cup tahini
3 tablespoons fresh lemon juice
1 large garlic clove, minced
1½ teaspoons sugar
⅛ teaspoon salt

⅛ teaspoon freshly ground
  pepper
⅛ teaspoon ground cumin
¼ cup vegetable oil
2 plum tomatoes, cut into
  wedges
1 kirby or small cucumber, sliced
1 onion, thinly sliced

1) In a medium bowl, combine the contents of the falafel mix with 1⅓ cups water (check the box, as some brands may vary). Let stand for 10 minutes.

2) Meanwhile, rinse and dry the lettuce. Arrange on a platter or 4 plates. In a small bowl, make the dressing by whisking together the tahini, lemon juice, garlic, sugar, salt, pepper, cumin, and 1½ tablespoons water.

3) Form the falafel into patties no thicker than ½ inch and about 2 inches in diameter. Heat 2 tablespoons oil in a large nonstick skillet over medium-high heat. Add the falafel in 2 batches and cook, turning, until brown and crisp on both sides, about 2 minutes each side. Drain on paper towels.

4) Arrange the falafel on top of the lettuce. Garnish with the tomatoes, cucumber, and onion. Drizzle the dressing over the salad. Serve at once.

Hominy Grits 'n Eggs

Canned hominy adds a corny taste and texture to the classic Southern combination of grits and eggs. Here the eggs are poached right on top of the hominy. This makes a simple, appealing brunch dish when accompanied by a tossed green salad or fresh fruit. Hominy is usually found in most supermarkets near the canned corn or next to the beans. If unavailable, it may be left out.   ***Makes 4 servings***

1 (14½-ounce) can white hominy, rinsed and drained
1 tablespoon butter
1 jalapeño pepper, seeded and minced
1 large garlic clove, minced
¼ teaspoon dried rosemary

¼ teaspoon salt
¾ cup old-fashioned grits
5 eggs
¼ cup shredded sharp Cheddar cheese
2 tablespoons chopped chives, scallion greens, or cilantro

1) In a large nonstick skillet, combine the hominy, butter, jalapeño pepper, garlic, rosemary, and salt. Add 2½ cups water and bring to a boil. Pour the grits in gradually, whisking to avoid lumps. Reduce the heat to medium-low and cook, covered, until the grits start to thicken, 5 to 7 minutes.

2) Whisk again to break up any lumps. One at a time, crack the eggs and gently drop onto the hominy, keeping the edges as separate as possible. Cover tightly and cook until the whites are set and no longer translucent, about 15 minutes. Turn off the heat, sprinkle with the cheese, and let stand, covered, until it is melted, about 1 minute. Sprinkle with the chives and serve immediately.

Marinated Portobello Mushroom Steaks

Meaty and rich, portobello mushrooms are the steak of the vegetable kingdom. These Asian-flavored mushrooms are sliced, marinated, and sautéed, then complemented with boy choy and homemade croutons for a delightful and elegant meal in a dish. **Makes 3 servings**

⅓ cup rice wine vinegar
¼ cup soy sauce
¼ cup vegetable oil
2 teaspoons grated fresh ginger
½ to 1 teaspoon hot chili oil, or to taste
2 large portobello mushrooms, stems removed, caps sliced ¾ inch thick

1 small red or yellow bell pepper, cut into ½-inch dice
2 large scallions, cut into 1-inch pieces
3 slices of firm-textured white bread, crusts removed
1 head of bok choy, cut into 2-inch pieces
1 teaspoon sesame seeds

1) In a medium bowl, combine the rice vinegar, soy sauce, 2 tablespoons of the vegetable oil, ginger, and hot oil. Add the sliced mushrooms, toss gently, and let marinate for 15 minutes.

2) Drain off and reserve the marinade. In a large heavy skillet, preferably cast-iron, cook the mushrooms, bell pepper, and scallions over medium-high heat, turning with tongs occasionally, until the mushrooms are tender, 5 to 7 minutes. Pour the mushrooms and vegetables into a bowl, cover, and set aside in a warm place.

3) Brush the bread lightly with the remaining vegetable oil. Cook in the skillet over medium-high heat, turning, until each side is brown and crisp, 3 to 5 minutes total. Remove from the heat and set aside.

4) Add the bok choy and remaining marinade to the skillet. Cook over medium-high heat, stirring frequently with tongs, just until the bok choy is slightly wilted, about 3 minutes.

5) To serve, cut the toasts diagonally into 4 triangles each. Place the bok choy on a plate or platter and top with the mushroom mixture. Arrange the boy choy and croutons around the edge and sprinkle the sesame seeds over the mushrooms. Serve immediately.

Fresh Mango Chutney and Brie Tortillas

Mangoes should be a bit soft to the touch when they are ripe. A ripe mango can easily be peeled by slicing four sides off the pit: two large, two small. Run a soup spoon between the skin and the flesh to separate.

For a smoky-tasting alternative, cook the tortillas over a gas range or grill. Lay them directly over the flame, turning quickly with tongs the minute they puff up and leaving them for just a few seconds on the second side. **Makes 4 servings**

8 (7-inch) flour tortillas
1 teaspoon vegetable oil
¼ cup thinly sliced shallots
1 teaspoon mustard seeds
2 ripe mangoes, peeled and
  thinly sliced

Pinch of crushed hot red pepper
2 teaspoons red wine vinegar
6 ounces Brie, at room
  temperature, rind removed,
  sliced into 8 thin strips

1) Preheat the oven to 200 degrees F. Heat a large cast-iron skillet over high heat. One at a time, place each tortilla in the dry skillet. When it starts to puff, about 1 minute, turn it over and cook the other side for about 30 seconds. Repeat with remaining tortillas. Wrap in foil and hold in oven.

2) Reduce the heat to medium and heat the oil. Add the shallots and cook, stirring frequently, until they are softened and translucent, 2 to 3 minutes. Add the mustard seeds; stir until they begin to pop, 1 to 2 minutes. Add the mango slices and hot pepper. Cook, stirring frequently, just until the mango is warm, about 1 minute. Stir in the vinegar.

3) Remove half the tortillas from the oven. Lay them on the counter. Place 1 strip of Brie on each tortilla, one-third up from the bottom. Spoon about 3 tablespoons of the fresh mango chutney on top of the Brie; roll the tortillas up tightly. Wrap the rolled tortillas in foil and return to the oven. Repeat with the remaining tortillas, Brie, and chutney. Serve at once.

Potato and Parsnip Fritters with Apple Horseradish Cream

Here is a variation on my grandmother's potato pancakes, made easy by grating the potatoes, parsnips, and onion in a food processor. For those on a diet, low-fat or nonfat sour cream works well in this recipe. Serve with sliced apples or a colorful fruit salad. **Makes 4 servings**

½ cup applesauce
¼ cup sour cream
1 tablespoon drained white
  horseradish
4 medium Idaho baking potatoes
  (2 pounds), peeled and
  shredded
4 medium parsnips, peeled and
  shredded

2 medium onions, grated
2 eggs
1 cup flour
1¼ teaspoons salt
1 teaspoon sugar
½ teaspoon freshly ground
  pepper
¼ cup oil

1) Preheat the oven to 200 degrees F. Make the horseradish cream by mixing together the applesauce, sour cream, and horseradish.

2) Place the shredded potatoes in a colander and, using your hands, squeeze out as much liquid as possible. Place in a kitchen towel and squeeze out as much liquid as possible again, then put the potatoes in a large bowl. Add the parsnips, onions, eggs, flour, salt, sugar, and pepper. Stir to mix well.

3) In a large heavy skillet, heat 2 tablespoons of the oil over medium-high heat. Drop the batter into the skillet by heaping tablespoons, pressing down to flatten the fritters. Cook in batches, adding extra oil as necessary, until they are a rich brown color, about 3 minutes on each side. As they are finished, place the fritters on a platter in the oven. Serve as soon as possible, accompanied with the horseradish cream.

Tempeh Burgers with Satay Sauce

Tempeh, *originally from Indonesia, is a soy product like tofu. But unlike tofu, its firm, nutty texture lends itself perfectly to vegetable burgers. Tempeh burgers have fifty percent more protein than burgers made of beef and are cholesterol free. Tempeh can be found next to the tofu in the produce department of the supermarket. For this recipe it is served with a satay peanut sauce. Sprouts and grated carrots go well on this burger.* **Makes 4 servings**

⅓ cup unsalted dry-roasted peanuts
1 large Vidalia or other sweet onion, sliced
3 tablespoons soy sauce
3 tablespoons lemon juice, preferably fresh
1½ tablespoons ground coriander
1 tablespoon packed brown sugar
1 large garlic clove, peeled and left whole
¼ to ½ teaspoon cayenne, to taste
4 hamburger rolls or English muffins, split in half and toasted
8 leaves of green leaf lettuce or half a bunch of arugula, tough ends removed
2 (8-ounce) packages tempeh
3 tablespoons vegetable oil

1) In a food processor, combine the peanuts, 1 slice of onion, the soy sauce, lemon juice, ground coriander, brown sugar, garlic, cayenne, and 2 tablespoons water. Puree until smooth. Set the satay sauce aside.

2) Set the bottoms of the toasted buns on 4 plates. Top each with one-fourth of the lettuce or arugula.

3) Cut each tempeh rectangle in half. In a large skillet, heat the oil over medium-high heat. Add the remaining onion slices and cook, stirring occasionally, for 2 minutes. Add the tempeh and cook, turning once, until warmed through, about 2 minutes each side. Reduce the heat to medium-low.

4) Spoon 1 tablespoon of the satay sauce on top of each burger; turn the burgers over and spoon another tablespoon on top of the second side. Add any remaining sauce to the pan, cover, and simmer 2 minutes. Place the tempeh burgers with some onion on the lettuce-lined buns. Top with the second half of the bun. Serve immediately.

Moroccan Tomatoes Stuffed with Eggplant

This summer dish should be *served with plenty of bread. The eggplant can be roasted a day ahead.*

Makes 4 servings

2 large eggplants
2 large beefsteak tomatoes
1¼ teaspoons salt
1 plum tomato, seeded and chopped
3 tablespoons extra-virgin olive oil
1 medium onion, chopped

5 garlic cloves, minced
1 teaspoon paprika
1 teaspoon ground coriander
1 teaspoon ground cumin
2 tablespoons fresh lemon juice
2 tablespoons chopped parsley
Freshly ground pepper

1) Preheat the oven to 425 degrees F. Pierce the eggplants several times with a fork, wrap in foil, and roast until soft, about 1 hour. Remove from the oven and let stand until cool enough to handle. Then cut lengthwise in half and scoop out the flesh with a large spoon; discard the skin and seeds. Chop the eggplant.

2) Prepare the beefsteak tomatoes by cutting them in half through the middle. With a spoon, scoop out and discard the seeds; scoop out and reserve any tomato in the center. Sprinkle the cavities with ¼ teaspoon salt and turn the tomatoes upside down on a rack. Chop the scooped out tomato and add it to the chopped plum tomato. Set aside in a small bowl.

3) In a medium skillet, heat 2 tablespoons of the oil over medium heat. Add the onion and cook until softened and translucent, about 5 minutes. Add the garlic, paprika, coriander, cumin, and remaining 1 teaspoon salt and cook for 1 minute to toast the spices.

4) Add the chopped eggplant and tomato to the onion-spice mixture. Cook over medium-high heat until any liquid evaporates, 2 to 3 minutes. Remove from the heat and stir in the remaining 1 tablespoon oil, the lemon juice, and 1 tablespoon of the parsley. Season with additional salt and pepper to taste.

5) Turn the tomatoes upright. If their tops are not straight, cut a small piece off the bottom to adjust. Place each tomato in the middle of a plate. Fill each with one-fourth of the eggplant salad, mounding it high. Sprinkle the remaining parsley over the top of the tomatoes and the plates. Serve at room temperature or cold.

Whole Wheat Cinnamon French Toast with Cider Maple Sauce and Raisins

This unique French toast *makes a great brunch or breakfast-as-dinner. To reduce the fat even further, use a nonstick pan and vegetable cooking spray in place of the butter and oil.*   **Makes 4 servings**

2 whole eggs
2 egg whites
1 cup milk
8 slices of whole wheat bread
2 tablespoons sugar
2 teaspoons cinnamon
1 tablespoon butter

1 tablespoon vegetable oil
1½ cups apple cider
¼ teaspoon grated orange zest
⅓ cup maple syrup
⅓ cup raisins
Pinch of ground cloves

1) Preheat the oven to 180 degrees F. Break the whole eggs into a 2-cup glass measure. Add the egg whites. With a fork or small whisk, beat lightly, then blend in the milk. Pour one-fourth of the liquid into each of 4 shallow bowls. Place 1 slice of bread in each bowl and turn until completely coated, about 30 seconds. Add a second piece of bread to each bowl and turn until both pieces are well coated.

2) Mix together the sugar and cinnamon. In a large nonstick skillet, melt ½ tablespoon of the butter in ½ tablespoon of the oil over medium-high heat. When the skillet is hot, use a metal spatula to carefully add the bread. Sprinkle the top slice with 1 teaspoon cinnamon-sugar. When the first side is well browned, 3 to 5 minutes, turn and cook the other side until it is well browned, crisp, and firm, about 2 minutes. Remove the French toast to a platter in the oven. Add the remaining oil and butter or spray the skillet with more vegetable oil. Repeat with the remaining bread.

3) Pour the cider and orange zest into the skillet. Boil until the cider is reduced to about ½ cup. Stir in the maple syrup, raisins, and cloves. Cook for 1 minute. Serve the French toast with a little sauce and raisins spooned on top.

Zucchini Feta Fritters

This is a variation on a
traditional Turkish recipe from Ayla Algar's Classic Turkish
Cooking. *These savory cakes are crisp on the outside and soft and
chewy on the inside. They are superb accompanied by a salad
or ripe tomatoes and chopped Greek olives. A colander set on top
of a bowl allows both the yogurt and zucchini to shed excess liquid.*

Makes 3 to 4 servings

¾ cup plain yogurt
1 pound zucchini
1 teaspoon salt
⅓ cup chopped cilantro or
   parsley
¼ cup feta cheese

2 eggs, lightly beaten
1 small onion, chopped
2 tablespoons flour
¼ teaspoon cayenne
3 tablespoons olive oil

1) Place a coffee filter or paper towel in a colander and spoon the yogurt
inside. Set the colander over a bowl and let stand for 15 to 20 minutes to
allow the yogurt to drip and thicken. Remove the yogurt to a small bowl.

2) In a food processor or on the large holes of a hand grater, shred the
zucchini. Toss with the salt and let sit in the colander placed over a bowl
20 to 30 minutes. Remove to a kitchen towel and squeeze out extra liquid.
Place in a medium bowl with the cilantro, feta cheese, eggs, onion, flour,
and cayenne. Mix well.

3) In a large nonstick skillet, heat the oil to medium-high. Add the
zucchini batter in heaping tablespoons, pressing down with the back of
a spoon, until the fritters are ½ inch thick. Cook in batches on both sides,
until crisp and brown, 2 to 3 minutes each side. Serve with a dollop of
the thickened yogurt.

The Vegetarian Stew Pot

Meat stews do not have a corner on the stew market. In fact, the following vegetable stews have numerous advantages over traditional meat stews. They are quicker cooking, more economical and varied, loaded with contrasting tastes and color, yet lower in fat and cholesterol.

But are they satisfying? After all, we enjoy stews for the same reason we crave soups, to placate our hunger with comforting, soul-satisfying food. Happily, this international array of stews, served alone in a bowl or accompanied with some bread or rice, hits the spot. For that reason, many of these dishes have become household staples for both myself and my students.

59

Stews are simple to prepare. Most cook quickly on top of the stove in a medium stew pot, which might be a large saucepan, a Dutch oven, or a flameproof casserole. Many start with a small amount of onion cooked in a little oil. The vegetables and grains are added with seasoning and liquid, like tomatoes or stock. The stew may be thickened simply with a touch of flour, either before or after the vegetables are added. Lastly, they simmer on the stove, to cook the vegetables and marry the flavors. How long the stew cooks will depend greatly on the size you cut the vegetables, so use the visual cues given in the recipes as a guide. It may help to remember that stewed vegetables are often cooked a little softer than stir-fried or steamed vegetables.

Most of these quickly prepared stews make good weekday eating, but you can also cook them at your leisure on the weekend and reheat them in the microwave after work. That's because stews are usually just as good, or even better, the next day. In addition, when unexpected company arrives, many of these recipes can be easily stretched by serving them over rice, pasta, potatoes, or couscous.

Vegetable stews provide amusing, unusual combinations as well as variations on familiar themes. Tex-Mex chili is transformed when hot spices are paired with sweet winter squash in Acorn Squash

and Red Bean Chili, or when "meaty" black beans meet creamy cheese in Quick Black Bean Chili with Goat Cheese. And in the summer, Vegetables à la Grecque, or Chickpeas with Lemony Tomato Sauce will cool the hottest night. Barley and Shiitake Stew is lightly perfumed with ginger and tamari, while fiery chipotle peppers add the smoke—and the heat—to Smoky Slow-Cooked Beans with Cumin. And peanut butter and coconut milk make a richly flavored sauce for Indonesian Green Beans and Tofu in Peanut Sauce.

Despite the exotic-sounding names, all the ingredients called for can be purchased at most supermarkets. In fact, many of these stews use canned cooked beans and tomatoes to help get dinner on the table fast.

Acorn Squash and
Red Bean Chili

Serve this unique low-fat chili
on its own, or with rice, tortilla chips, or corn bread.

Makes 6 servings

1 acorn squash (1½ pounds)
1½ tablespoons vegetable oil
1 medium onion, chopped
1 green bell pepper, cut into
  ½-inch dice
2 tablespoons chili powder
1½ tablespoons ground cumin
½ teaspoon cayenne
⅛ teaspoon cinnamon
3 (14½-ounce) cans stewed
  tomatoes

1 (14½-ounce) can dark red
  kidney beans, rinsed and
  drained
1 tablespoon cider vinegar
½ teaspoon salt
8 pitted olives, sliced
¼ cup sour cream
⅓ cup chopped scallion greens

1) With a large knife, carefully quarter the acorn squash. Remove the seeds and peel. Cut the squash into ½-inch cubes.

2) In a large stew pot or flameproof casserole, heat the oil over medium heat. Add the onion and bell pepper and cook, stirring occasionally, until the onion is softened and translucent, 3 to 5 minutes.

3) Stir in the squash, chili powder, cumin, cayenne, cinnamon, tomatoes and their juices, beans, vinegar, and salt. Cover and cook until the squash is tender but still holds its shape, about 20 minutes. Season with additional salt and cayenne to taste. Serve in bowls topped with the olives, sour cream, and scallion greens.

Quick Black Bean Chili
with Goat Cheese

To turn this into instant party *fare, serve with a variety of colorful accompaniments: tortilla chips or corn bread, diced red onion, avocado, and tomato.*

Makes 4 to 6 servings

1½ tablespoons vegetable oil
1 small red onion, chopped
1 medium green bell pepper,
  chopped
3 garlic cloves, minced
2 teaspoons ground cumin
2 teaspoons chili powder
⅛ teaspoon crushed hot red
  pepper
1 (28-ounce) can crushed
  tomatoes

2 (15-ounce) cans black beans,
  rinsed and drained
1 (4-ounce) can mild chopped
  green chiles, drained
½ teaspoon salt
¼ cup chopped cilantro
  (optional)
3 ounces goat cheese, crumbled
  or cut into small pieces

1) In a medium pot, heat the oil over medium heat. Add the red onion and green pepper. Cook, stirring frequently, until the onion is softened and translucent, 3 to 5 minutes. Add the garlic, cumin, chili powder, and hot pepper. Cook, stirring constantly, for 1 minute to toast the spices.

2) Stir in the tomatoes, black beans, chiles, and salt. Simmer for 15 minutes. Season with additional hot pepper and salt to taste, bearing in mind that the goat cheese is salty.

3) To serve, ladle into warm bowls. Sprinkle the cilantro and goat cheese on top.

Smoky Slow-Cooked Beans
with Cumin

This is a foolproof way to
*make perfect dried beans from scratch. Serve these tasty beans
ladled into bowls simply by themselves or, better yet, topped with
sour cream, cheese, and salsa, or with chopped tomatoes and
cilantro. Or roll them up in tortillas with salsa and sour cream or
yogurt.*   ***Makes 6 to 8 servings***

1 pound dried black beans
2 to 4 dried chipotle chiles or
   minced canned chipotles or
   ½ to 1 teaspoon cayenne, to
   taste
3 tablespoons olive oil

2 large Spanish onions, chopped
2 teaspoons cumin seeds
10 garlic cloves, chopped
2 teaspoons salt
2 teaspoons balsamic vinegar

1) Rinse the beans and pick them over to remove any grit. Put them in a
large stew pot or flameproof casserole and add enough cold water to
cover the beans by at least 2 inches. Let soak overnight. Drain the beans into
a colander. Rinse the pot and wipe dry.

2) If you are using dried chipotle chiles, cover with boiling water and
soak until softened, about 30 minutes. Discard the stems, seeds, and ribs.
Finely chop the chiles.

3) Heat the olive oil in the stew pot over medium heat. Add the onions
and cook, stirring occasionally, until they are softened and translucent,
about 5 minutes. Add the cumin seeds and cook, stirring, 1 to 2 minutes
longer, to toast lightly.

4) Add the beans, chipotle chiles, and garlic. Cover with 1 inch of water
and bring to a boil over high heat. Reduce the heat to medium and cook,
partially covered, adding a little water as necessary to keep the beans just
covered, until the beans are soft, about 1 hour.

5) Puree about one-fourth of the beans with liquid in a food processor
until smooth. Return to the pot, stir in the salt and vinegar, and serve.

Italian Artichoke, Fennel, and White Bean Ambrosia

Accompany this stew with a good bread, such as sourdough whole wheat. The frozen artichoke hearts can be defrosted overnight in the refrigerator or in the microwave, unwrapped and covered, for about 3 minutes.

Makes 4 to 6 servings

1 (10-ounce) package frozen
   artichoke hearts, thawed
6 Calamata or 4 Greek black
   olives, pitted and chopped
3 tablespoons olive oil
3 garlic cloves, minced
2 teaspoons capers, drained
Pinch of crushed hot red pepper
2 medium fennel bulbs or
   3 celery ribs

1 large onion, sliced
2 (14½-ounce) cans stewed
   tomatoes
1 (14½-ounce) can white beans,
   rinsed and drained
⅛ teaspoon salt
3 tablespoons grated Parmesan
   cheese

1) In a medium bowl, mix the artichoke hearts with the olives, 1 tablespoon olive oil, garlic, capers, and hot peppers. Marinate for 20 minutes.

2) Pull off some of the dark green fennel leaves (if they are included with the bulbs), chop 1 tablespoon, and set aside. Remove and discard the outer stalks from the fennel bulbs and trim the root ends. Cut the bulbs into cubes about the size of the artichoke hearts. If using celery, cut into 1-inch pieces.

3) In a medium stew pot, heat the remaining 2 tablespoons oil over medium heat. Add the onion and fennel. Cook until the onion is translucent, about 5 minutes. Add the stewed tomatoes, cover, and cook for an additional 5 minutes. Add the beans, salt, and marinated artichoke hearts. Cover and cook until the fennel is tender but not mushy, 5 to 10 minutes. Serve in bowls, sprinkled with the Parmesan cheese and fennel leaves.

Barley and Shiitake Stew with Ginger and Tamari

This is a variation on the classic combination of mushrooms and barley. If you want to turn it into a thick soup, just reduce the barley by one-third cup. Barley is located next to the dried beans, and tamari is with the Asian foods, near the soy sauce, in the supermarket. Tamari is a soy product, like soy sauce, but it has a rounder, more complex flavor.

Makes 4 servings

2 tablespoons olive oil
⅔ cup sliced shallots or onion
¼ pound white button
  mushrooms, sliced
¼ pound shiitake or other wild
  mushrooms, stems removed
  and caps sliced

1 teaspoon tamari or
  1½ teaspoons soy sauce
1 teaspoon grated fresh ginger
1 cup pearl barley
1 (14½-ounce) can vegetable
  broth
1 tablespoon chopped parsley

1) In a medium stew pot, heat the oil over medium heat. Add the shallots, white mushrooms, and shiitakes. Cook, stirring frequently, until the shallots are starting to brown, about 7 minutes. Remove to a small bowl.

2) Add the tamari, ginger, barley, broth, and 3½ cups water to the pot. Bring to a boil, reduce the heat to medium-low, cover, and cook for 20 minutes. Stir in the mushroom-shallot mixture and continue to cook, covered, until the barley is tender, about 20 minutes longer.

3) Ladle into bowls and garnish with the parsley. Serve immediately.

Beans Puttanesca on Polenta

Beans are presented here in a
*spicy tomato sauce atop creamy carefree polenta, Italian
cornmeal mush. Coarse or stone-ground cornmeal is available in
some supermarkets and in all health and specialty food stores.*

Makes 4 to 6 servings

1 (28-ounce) can crushed
  tomatoes
1 tablespoon drained capers
12 Greek black olives, pitted and
  chopped
½ teaspoon crushed hot red
  pepper
1 (14½-ounce) can black beans,
  rinsed and drained

1½ cups yellow cornmeal,
  preferably stone-ground
¾ teaspoon salt
1½ tablespoons butter
½ cup grated Parmesan cheese
2 tablespoons chopped parsley

1) Preheat the oven to 200 degrees F. In a medium, preferably nonstick, stew pot, combine the tomatoes, capers, olives, hot pepper, and beans. Cook over medium heat for 8 minutes, stirring occasionally. Remove to a covered ovenproof bowl. Place in the oven to keep warm.

2) Rinse out the stew pot with water. Pour the water, cornmeal, and salt into the pot. Bring to a boil, reduce the heat to low, and cook, stirring frequently with a wooden spoon, until the cornmeal starts to pull away from the sides of the pot, about 15 minutes. Stir in the butter and cheese and stir until melted.

3) Immediately place a mound of polenta on each plate. With a spoon, make an indentation in the center of the polenta. Ladle the beans puttanesca on top. Sprinkle with parsley and serve immediately.

Butternut Squash and Swiss Chard Stew

For an extra treat, save the squash seeds; they make a tasty and nutritious topping. Simply dry, then toss them very lightly in olive oil. Toast in a 375 degree F oven (or toaster oven) until crispy, about 15 minutes.

Makes 4 to 6 servings

1 butternut squash (2¼ pounds)
1 bunch of Swiss chard (about 1½ pounds)
¼ cup fruity olive oil
3 medium leeks (white and tender green), halved lengthwise, well rinsed, and sliced
8 garlic cloves, sliced

½ teaspoon salt
½ teaspoon crushed hot red pepper
¼ teaspoon dried thyme leaves
¼ teaspoon dried sage
4 plum tomatoes, quartered
¼ cup chopped parsley
4 lemon wedges

1) Prepare the butternut squash by cutting crosswise into 4 pieces. Cut each piece in half through the center and scrape out the seeds and pulp. Peel carefully and then cut the flesh into 1½-inch chunks.

2) To prepare the Swiss chard, separate the green leaves from the center ribs. Stack the leaves, roll, and cut into strips. Coarsely chop the stems.

3) In a large stew pot or flameproof casserole, heat the olive oil over medium heat. Add the leeks, garlic, salt, hot pepper, thyme, and sage. Cook until the leeks just begin to soften, about 3 minutes.

4) Add the squash, tomatoes, and ⅓ cup water. Bring to a boil, reduce the heat to medium, and cover. Cook until the squash is soft but not mushy, about 10 minutes.

5) Add the Swiss chard and parsley. Cook, covered, until the Swiss chard is wilted but still bright green, 2 to 3 minutes. Season with additional salt and pepper to taste. Serve in bowls accompanied by the lemon wedges.

Chickpeas with Lemony Tomato Sauce

Serve this flavorful dish at
*room temperature or chilled, with plenty of pita bread and a
dish of plain yogurt on the side.* **Makes 3 to 4 servings**

2 medium leeks (white and
   tender green)
2 lemons
1½ tablespoons olive oil
1½ teaspoons ground coriander
1 teaspoon ground cumin
¾ teaspoon fennel seed
½ teaspoon salt
¼ to ½ teaspoon cayenne, to
   taste

1 (14½-ounce) can diced
   tomatoes, with their juices
1 (15-ounce) can chickpeas
   (garbanzo beans), rinsed
   and drained
12 oil-cured Mediterranean
   olives, pitted and chopped
4 pita breads, cut into wedges

1) Trim the leeks, slit them lengthwise in half, and rinse well under running water to remove any sand or grit. Coarsely chop the leeks.

2) Grate the zest from 1 lemon and squeeze 1 tablespoon juice from half of the same lemon; set aside separately. Cut the second lemon into wedges.

3) In a large nonreactive saucepan or flameproof casserole, heat the oil over medium heat. Add the leeks, coriander, cumin, fennel, salt, and cayenne. Cook, stirring often, until the leeks are soft, about 5 minutes.

4) Add the tomatoes with their liquid, the chickpeas, olives, and lemon zest. Bring to a boil. Reduce the heat to medium and cook, stirring occasionally, until the tomato sauce is very thick, about 15 minutes. Remove from the heat and stir in the lemon juice. Serve at room temperature or cover and refrigerate until chilled, at least 2 hours. Serve with lemon wedges and pita bread.

Eggplant and Potato Curry

Makes 4 to 6 servings

1 medium eggplant (about
   1¼ pounds), cut into ¾-inch
   cubes
1 tablespoon salt
1 tablespoon butter
2 tablespoons vegetable oil
2 medium onions, sliced
1 tablespoon curry powder
6 medium new potatoes, cut into
   small cubes

2 tablespoons balsamic or red
   wine vinegar
1 tablespoon plus 1 teaspoon
   brown sugar
1 tablespoon tomato paste
1½ cups fresh or frozen peas
⅔ cup plain yogurt

1) In a colander, toss the eggplant with 2 teaspoons of the salt. Let stand 20 to 30 minutes to drain; then rinse under cold running water and squeeze dry.

2) In a large stew pot, melt the butter in the oil over medium heat. Add the onions, eggplant, curry powder, and remaining 1 teaspoon salt. Cook, stirring occasionally, until the eggplant is soft, about 8 minutes. Add the potatoes and continue to cook, stirring occasionally, until the potatoes are roughly half cooked, about 8 minutes longer.

3) In a medium bowl, blend the vinegar, brown sugar, and tomato paste with 1½ cups water. Stir into the stew pot, cover, and cook until the potatoes are just tender and the sauce has thickened, about 5 minutes. Stir in the peas and cover again. Reduce the heat to low and cook until the peas are tender if fresh or warmed through if frozen, 2 to 5 minutes. Spoon into bowls. Top with a dollop of yogurt.

Indonesian Green Beans and Tofu in Peanut Sauce

Even those not crazy about tofu will flip for this dish, which is terrific over rice. Unsweetened canned coconut milk can be found in the Asian section of the supermarket.

Makes 3 to 4 servings

½ pound green beans, cut in half crosswise
⅔ cup chunky peanut butter
½ cup unsweetened canned coconut milk
1 tablespoon plus 1 teaspoon soy sauce
2 teaspoons curry powder

½ teaspoon salt
Pinch of cayenne
1 (16-ounce) container firm tofu, well drained and cut into 1-inch cubes
6 scallions, cut into 2-inch lengths

1) In a medium stew pot, bring ⅔ cup water to a boil over high heat. Add the green beans and reduce the heat to medium. Cook, covered, for 3 minutes.

2) In a small bowl, thoroughly whisk together the peanut butter, coconut milk, soy sauce, curry powder, salt, cayenne, and another ⅔ cup water. Pour over the green beans. Add the tofu and scallions.

3) Cook, covered, stirring once or twice, until the tofu is warmed through and the sauce has thickened a bit, 5 to 7 minutes. Season with additional salt and cayenne to taste. Serve in bowls as is or over plain boiled rice.

Rice and Red Lentil Stew with Cauliflower and Peas

This is an adaptation of a
traditional stew featured in Yamuna Devi's The Art of Indian
Vegetarian Cooking. *Red lentils can be found in health food stores
as well as in the dried bean section of many supermarkets.*

Makes 4 to 6 servings

1 tablespoon vegetable oil
2 large leeks (white and tender
   green), well rinsed and sliced
1½ teaspoons ground coriander
1½ teaspoons ground cumin
1½ teaspoons dry mustard
1 teaspoon turmeric
¼ teaspoon cayenne

¾ cup long-grain white rice
1½ teaspoons salt
½ cup red lentils or ordinary
   brown lentils
½ medium head of cauliflower,
   cut into 1-inch florets
½ cup fresh or frozen peas
2 tablespoons butter

1) In a medium stew pot, heat the oil over medium heat. Add the leeks, coriander, cumin, mustard, turmeric, and cayenne, stirring constantly to toast the spices, for 1 minute.

2) Add the rice, salt, and 4¼ cups water. Bring to a boil over high heat. Stir in the lentils. Reduce the heat to medium, cover, and cook until the rice and lentils are just tender, about 20 minutes for red lentils, 35 minutes if you are using brown lentils.

3) Add the cauliflower, raise the heat to high, and continue to cook, covered, stirring occasionally, for 5 minutes. Add the peas and cook until they are warmed through and the stew has an oatmeal-like consistency, about 5 minutes longer. Add the butter, stirring until it melts. Serve hot in bowls.

Creamy Spinach and Red Potato Stew

Frozen spinach can be defrosted overnight in the refrigerator or in a covered bowl for about 2 minutes in the microwave. Squeeze it thoroughly dry in a kitchen towel or in a piece of cheesecloth. **Makes 4 servings**

12 small red potatoes
  (2½ pounds), scrubbed and
  halved
1 (14½-ounce) can vegetable
  broth
2 garlic cloves, minced
2 tablespoons unsalted butter, at
  room temperature

2 tablespoons flour
½ cup half-and-half
1 (10-ounce) package frozen
  chopped spinach, thawed
  and squeezed dry
¼ teaspoon freshly ground
  pepper
¼ teaspoon grated nutmeg

1) In a large saucepan or flameproof casserole, combine the potatoes with the broth and garlic. Bring to a boil, cover, and cook until the potatoes are cooked through but not mushy, about 15 minutes.

2) In a small bowl, blend the butter and flour to a paste. Pour the half-and-half over the potatoes and bring to a boil. Stir pieces of the butter-flour mixture into the pot. Return to a boil, stirring until the sauce is thickened and smooth. Add the spinach and cook, stirring, 1 to 2 minutes. Season with the pepper and nutmeg. Serve immediately in bowls.

Tomato and Escarole Stew

Prepare this garlicky stew when garden tomatoes are at their peak. Serve with wedges of peasant bread for dunking.

Makes 4 servings

¼ cup olive oil
2 medium onions, sliced
7 garlic cloves, minced
½ cup medium- or long-grain
  white rice
4 large ripe tomatoes, peeled,
  seeded, and coarsely
  chopped

1 teaspoon salt
1 large head of escarole,
  coarsely chopped
¾ teaspoon freshly ground
  pepper
¼ cup grated Parmesan cheese

1) In a large saucepan, heat the oil over medium heat. Add the onions and garlic. Cook until the onion is softened and translucent, 3 to 5 minutes. Add the rice and cook, stirring, 1 to 2 minutes to coat with oil.

2) Add the tomatoes, salt, and 2 cups water. Cover and cook over medium heat 10 minutes.

3) Add the escarole and cook until the rice is tender and the escarole is wilted, 5 to 10 minutes. Stir in the pepper. Season with additional salt to taste. Serve in bowls, with the Parmesan cheese sprinkled on top.

Spicy South Indian Vegetable Curry

Despite the long list of ingredients, this colorful stew is a snap to prepare. Serve it on its own or with rice. Cool off the heat of the dish with a dollop of plain yogurt or yogurt mixed with chopped cucumber and onion, called raita. Unsweetened coconut milk can be found in cans in the Asian foods section of most supermarkets.

Makes 4 servings

1 tablespoon vegetable oil
1 onion, thickly sliced
2 large red potatoes, scrubbed
  and cut into ½-inch dice
½ teaspoon crushed hot red
  pepper
1 tablespoon mustard seeds
1½ tablespoons ground
  coriander
2 teaspoons ground cumin
¼ teaspoon cinnamon

½ teaspoon salt
1 (8-ounce) can stewed tomatoes
½ cup unsweetened coconut milk
¾ pound small turnips, peeled
  and thickly sliced
2 carrots, cut into 1-inch pieces
½ pound green beans, cut in half
  crosswise
1 cup fresh or frozen corn
  kernels

1) In a medium stew pot, heat the oil over medium heat. Add the onion and cook, stirring frequently, until it starts to brown, about 7 minutes. Add the potatoes, hot pepper, mustard seeds, coriander, cumin, cinnamon, and salt. Cook, stirring, until the spices are aromatic, 1 to 2 minutes.

2) Stir in the tomatoes and coconut milk. Cover and cook for 5 minutes. Add the turnips, carrots, and green beans. Continue to cook, covered, until the potatoes and turnips are tender, about 15 minutes.

3) Stir in the corn and cook until just tender, about 3 minutes. Serve hot.

Vegetable Goulash

Fresh, good-quality paprika makes all the difference in this chunky winter stew. Serve as is with crusty bread, over wide egg noodles, or with brown rice.

Makes 4 servings

1½ tablespoons vegetable oil
1 large onion, sliced
1 green bell pepper, cut into
  1-inch cubes
2 tablespoons sweet paprika,
  preferably Hungarian
⅛ teaspoon cayenne
1 teaspoon salt
1 (8-ounce) can tomato sauce
2 tablespoons dry red or white
  wine

½ teaspoon sugar
2 large red or Yukon gold
  potatoes, peeled and cut into
  1½-inch cubes
2 large plum tomatoes, coarsely
  chopped
3 medium parsnips, peeled and
  cut into 1-inch pieces
⅓ cup sour cream
1½ teaspoons flour
1½ tablespoons chopped parsley

1) In a medium stew pot, heat the oil over medium heat. Add the onion and bell pepper and cook, stirring occasionally, until the onion starts to brown, about 7 minutes.

2) Reduce the heat to low. Add the paprika, cayenne, and salt. Cook, stirring for 30 seconds to toast the spices. Immediately stir in the tomato sauce, wine, sugar, and 1 cup water.

3) Add the potatoes, tomatoes, and parsnips and bring to a boil. Reduce the heat to medium, cover, and cook until the potatoes are tender but not falling apart, 20 to 25 minutes.

4) In a small bowl, thoroughly blend the sour cream and flour until smooth. When the stew has finished cooking, ladle about 1 cup of the liquid into the sour cream and mix. Stir the sour cream mixture back into the stew pot. Cook until the sauce thickens a little, about 2 minutes. Ladle into bowls. Sprinkle the parsley on top.

Vegetables à la Grecque

This tart vegetable salad is superb marinated in the refrigerator overnight, then served in a bowl, garnished with Greek olives, and accompanied with whole-grain bread and fresh goat cheese. ***Makes 4 to 6 servings***

⅓ cup olive oil, preferably extra-
    virgin
⅓ cup fresh lemon juice
2 garlic cloves, minced
1 teaspoon salt
1 teaspoon fennel seeds
¾ teaspoon ground coriander
¾ teaspoon dried oregano

¾ teaspoon dried thyme leaves
¼ teaspoon freshly ground
    pepper
5 medium carrots, peeled
2 small zucchini
1 small head of cauliflower, cut
    into 1½-inch florets

1) In a large stew pot, combine 4 cups water with the olive oil, lemon juice, garlic, salt, fennel seeds, coriander, oregano, thyme, and pepper. Bring to a boil, reduce the heat to low, cover, and cook for 5 minutes.

2) Meanwhile, cut the carrots and zucchini in half lengthwise. Cut crosswise on a diagonal into 1-inch lengths.

3) Raise the heat to medium. Add the carrots to the poaching liquid. Cover and simmer for 5 minutes. Stir in the cauliflower, pressing it down so that as much as possible is covered. Cook, covered, 5 minutes. Place the zucchini on top of the other vegetables, cover, and cook for an additional 5 minutes.

4) Remove from the heat and let cool in the liquid. Marinate the vegetables still in their liquid in a plastic bag or container in the refrigerator overnight. Serve the vegetables chilled in some of the liquid or drained. Season with additional salt to taste before serving.

Yam and Wild Mushroom Stew

This dish is one of my favorite *vegetable stews because I love the way the sweet orange yams play off the dark woodsy mushrooms.* ***Makes 3 to 4 servings***

¼ cup boiling water
2 tablespoons dry sherry
3 large dried shiitake
  mushrooms
3 leeks (white and tender green),
  well rinsed and sliced
2 small yams, peeled and cut into
  1-inch cubes
¼ teaspoon salt
¼ teaspoon dried thyme leaves

½ pound fresh shiitake or other
  wild mushroom, stemmed,
  caps quartered
1 (14½-ounce) can vegetable
  broth
⅛ teaspoon pepper
2 tablespoons butter, at room
  temperature
2 tablespoons flour

1) In a small heatproof bowl, pour the boiling water and sherry over the dried mushrooms; let stand until softened, about 15 minutes. Cut off and discard the stems; chop the caps and set aside. Strain the soaking liquid through a paper towel–lined sieve or coffee filter; reserve the soaking liquid.

2) In a medium stew pot, combine the leeks, yams, salt, thyme, and ½ cup water. Cook over medium-high heat, partially covered, until the yams are tender when pierced with a fork and the water is almost evaporated, about 10 minutes.

3) Add the chopped dried and quartered fresh shiitake mushroom caps to the stew pot. Reduce the heat to medium and cook, stirring gently, until the mushrooms start to wilt, about 3 minutes.

4) Add the broth and pepper to the stew and bring to a boil. In a small bowl, blend the butter and flour into a paste. Gradually stir the butter-flour paste into the stew. Bring to a boil, stirring until the sauce thickens, 1 to 2 minutes. Serve in warm bowls.

Yukon Gold Potato and Sorrel Stew with Sweet Corn

If any of the ingredients for this tangy stew are hard to find, here are some substitutions: Sorrel, a lemon-flavored leafy green, may be replaced by any strong-flavored green, such as arugula or curly green endive, along with ¼ teaspoon grated lemon zest. The rich-tasting Yukon Gold potatoes, now widely available in supermarkets, can be replaced with any waxy red or white potatoes. **Makes 4 servings**

6 medium Yukon Gold potatoes (about 2 pounds), quartered
1 large onion, sliced
2 large garlic cloves, sliced
1 teaspoon salt
¼ teaspoon freshly ground pepper
1 (14½-ounce) can vegetable broth

2 cups milk
2 tablespoons butter, at room temperature
2 tablespoons flour
1 large bunch of sorrel, coarsely chopped (about 1½ cups)
1½ cups fresh or frozen corn kernels

1) In a large stew pot, combine the potatoes, onion, garlic, ½ teaspoon of the salt, the pepper, and the vegetable broth. Cook over medium-high heat, partially covered, until the potatoes are almost tender throughout and the liquid is almost evaporated, about 15 minutes.

2) Add the milk and remaining ½ teaspoon salt to the stew and bring to a boil over medium-high heat. In a small bowl, blend the butter and flour to a paste. Gradually stir the paste into the stew. Boil, stirring gently, until the stew thickens, about 1 minute.

3) Add the sorrel and corn. Cook 2 minutes and serve.

Zucchini Niçoise

This versatile stew is good warm or cold. It is excellent with bread or even tossed with pasta or over grains. Good-quality olives give a distinctive flavor to this dish. Niçoise olives can be found at most gourmet food shops. Oil-cured or Greek black olives, available in supermarkets, can be substituted. Be sure to pit them. To pit any type of olive, use a pitter or remove the pit easily by hand after you flatten the olive with a wooden spoon.

Makes 4 servings

¼ cup olive oil
1 small Spanish onion, diced
½ teaspoon dried thyme leaves
4 garlic cloves, sliced
1 red bell pepper, cut into 1-inch cubes
1 yellow bell pepper, cut into 1-inch cubes

4 medium zucchini, thickly sliced
1 pint cherry tomatoes, halved (about 2 cups)
½ cup pitted Niçoise olives
½ teaspoon salt
½ teaspoon freshly ground pepper
1 lemon, cut into wedges

1) In a medium stew pot, heat the oil over medium heat. Add the onion, thyme, and garlic and cook, stirring occasionally, until the onion is translucent, about 5 minutes.

2) Stir in the bell peppers, reduce the heat to medium-low, and cook, covered, stirring occasionally, for 10 minutes. Add the zucchini and cook, covered, until the zucchini are soft but not mushy, about 15 minutes.

3) Remove the stew pot from the heat. After 5 minutes, when the stew has cooled down a bit, gently stir in the cherry tomatoes, olives, salt, and pepper. Serve hot, at room temperature, or chilled, with lemon wedges.

Vegetarian Pasta

Pasta dishes may be the most popular vegetarian meals in America. The endless variety of shapes cook quickly, and they are a natural foil for vegetables, beans, and even some whole grains. Buckwheat and pasta, for example, are a traditional pairing. Pasta is always a hit with both adults and children, making it the perfect family meal. And when the pasta and the sauce are made in the same pot, it becomes the perfect one-pot meal as well.

There are a few secrets to cooking perfect pasta. First, to allow the pasta to cook quickly and evenly, use four quarts of water for every pound of pasta. To season the pasta, which is bland, salt should be added to the boiling water. Italians suggest

1½ tablespoons per four quarts of water, but many Americans prefer less. (Remember, only a small fraction of that amount is actually ingested.) Once the water comes to a rapid boil, add the pasta all at once to assure even cooking. A pot cover can be placed on top, slightly askew, just until the water returns to a boil to facilitate quicker cooking, but be sure to remove it at that point, or the water may boil over.

The hardest part of cooking pasta is to avoid overcooking it. Always test for doneness, using the cooking times given only as a guide. Most dried pasta cooks in 8 to 10 minutes. Begin testing when the minimum cooking time is reached. Use a slotted spoon or tongs to pull out a single piece of the pasta. Rinse briefly to cool if necessary, then taste it. It should be tender but not soft all the way through, yet still firm to the bite—what the Italians call "al dente." Immediately strain the pasta into a colander set in the sink. Remember that hot pasta cooks a little after it is drained, so when in doubt it is better to leave it a bit underdone.

Whether you've chosen a substantial dish, such as Fusilli with Lentil Sauce or Pesto Gnocchi with Vegetables, or a lighter pasta, such as Penne and Asparagus with Garlic-Tomato Vinaigrette or Spaghettini with Fennel, Currants, and Pine Nuts, it's

ONE-POT VEGETARIAN DISHES

important to toss the pasta and sauce together as soon as possible until evenly coated. Though not essential, serving pasta from the warm cooking pot or from a heated serving dish will keep it hot longer. A large serving bowl or platter can easily be heated by pouring hot tap water into it, draining it, and then wiping it dry. Pasta for cold dishes, like Summer Tortellini Salad or Szechuan Cold Sesame Noodles, should be rinsed briefly with cold water just after cooking and then drained well so that it doesn't stick together.

Most of the pasta dishes in this chapter are made with dried pasta, which is easily available, keeps in the cupboard, has a nice full body, and contains no cholesterol. Fresh pasta cooks very quickly, usually in 2 to 3 minutes, and has a more delicate texture. These days it can be found in the refrigerated section of most supermarkets. If you are using fresh, be sure to reduce the cooking time accordingly.

Buckwheat and Bow Ties with Browned Onions

Thiis is a recipe for kasha varnishkas, *a popular Eastern European Jewish dish. Kasha, another name for buckwheat groats, it sold in the Jewish or kosher food section of your supermarket or with the grains in health food stores. If possible, use coarse, rather than medium, buckwheat groats for this dish.* **Makes 4 servings**

2 tablespoons olive oil
3 medium onions, sliced
1 cup kasha, preferably coarse
1 (14½-ounce) can vegetable broth
⅓ cup chopped parsley

½ pound bow-tie pasta
Salt
1½ teaspoons butter
1 teaspoon freshly ground pepper

1) In a large pasta pot, heat the oil and onions over medium heat. Cook, stirring frequently, until the onions are well browned, about 10 minutes.

2) Add the kasha and stir to coat. Pour in the vegetable broth and ¼ cup water and bring to a boil. Reduce the heat to medium-low. Cover by pressing wax paper over the water, then covering again with the pot lid. Cook until the grain is done, from 5 minutes for medium kasha to 20 minutes for coarse. (It is fine if the kasha is a little undercooked, as it will continue to steam while the bow-tie pasta cooks.) Remove the kasha to a medium bowl, add the parsley, and fluff with a fork to separate the grains.

3) Rinse out the pot. Bring 4 quarts of salted water to a rapid boil. Add the bow ties and salt to taste. Cook until the pasta is tender but still firm, 8 to 12 minutes. Drain and return to the pot.

4) Add the butter and pepper and toss. Add the kasha. Warm over medium-high heat, stirring constantly while adding ¼ cup water, until warm, 2 to 3 minutes. Serve at once.

Fettuccine with Blue Cheese, Hazelnuts, and Green Beans

This is a lighter version of a very rich and decadent pasta recipe. Although any fettuccine is lovely, mixed spinach (green) and egg (white) fettuccine, readily found in supermarkets, is particularly pretty in this dish.

Makes 4 servings

¾ pound dried fettuccine
½ pound green beans, cut in half lengthwise (2 cups)
½ cup coarsely chopped hazelnuts or pecans
¼ cup heavy cream
1 cup milk

2 tablespoons chopped shallots
¼ teaspoon salt
½ teaspoon freshly ground pepper
¼ cup crumbled blue cheese, such as Danish, Roquefort, or Gorgonzola

1) In a large pasta pot, bring 4 quarts of salted water to a rapid boil. Add the fettuccine, blending it gently with a wooden spoon once it is in the pot to fit it all in. After 2 minutes, add the green beans and continue cooking, stirring occasionally, until the fettuccine is tender but still firm, 7 to 8 minutes longer. Drain the pasta and beans into a colander and rinse briefly under running water; drain well.

2) Carefully dry the pasta pot. Add the nuts to the dry pot and cook over medium heat, stirring constantly, for about 2 minutes, until they smell aromatic. Add the cream, milk, shallots, ¼ teaspoon salt, and pepper. Bring to a boil and boil for 1 minute.

3) Return the pasta and green beans to the pot. Immediately sprinkle in the blue cheese. Using tongs, toss over medium heat until the fettuccine and beans are warm and well coated with sauce, about 1 minute. Season with additional salt and freshly ground pepper to taste. Serve at once.

Fresh Fettuccine with Creamy Morel Sauce

This elegant and rich pasta dish makes a quick, romantic one-pot meal. It is my husband's favorite; so every spring we wait for fresh morels to come into season. They are a luxury, but well worth the occasional splurge, especially since half a pound serves four.

Makes 4 servings

½ pound fresh morel mushrooms
1 tablespoon butter
⅓ cup chopped shallots
1¼ cups heavy cream
1 tablespoon dry sherry
¼ teaspoon salt

¼ teaspoon freshly ground pepper
12 ounces fresh fettuccine
2 tablespoons grated Parmesan cheese
1 tablespoon chopped parsley

1) Quarter the morels lengthwise. Set them in a medium bowl of cold water. Swish them around gently with your hands, then pour off the dirt. Repeat. Place in a colander and gently run under cold water. Shake the colander to remove excess water.

2) In a large pasta pot, melt the butter over medium-low heat. Add the shallots and cook, stirring frequently, until soft and translucent, 2 to 3 minutes. Add the cream with about one-fourth of the morels. Bring to a boil and cook, stirring occasionally, until it reduces slightly, about 3 minutes. Add the sherry, salt, and pepper, reduce the heat to medium-low, and add the remaining morels. With a rubber spatula, scrape the sauce into a bowl. Cover and set aside in a warm place.

3) In a pasta pot, bring 3 quarts of salted water to a rapid boil. Add the fettuccine. Cook just until tender, about 3 minutes. Drain the pasta.

4) Reduce the heat to medium. Return the pasta to the pot. Pour in the morel sauce and toss over heat, until warmed through, about 30 seconds. Season with additional salt and pepper to taste. Serve immediately in warm bowls, sprinkled with the Parmesan cheese and parsley.

Fusilli with Lentil Sauce

This is an instant version of pasta with lentils, a traditional Italian dish rarely seen in America.

Makes 4 servings

¾ pound fusilli
1 cup fresh or frozen peas
2 carrots, peeled and thinly
  sliced
1 (16½-ounce) can lentil soup
3 garlic cloves, minced
3 tablespoons olive oil

¼ cup sliced scallion greens
2 tablespoons balsamic vinegar
¼ teaspoon salt
¼ teaspoon freshly ground
  pepper
⅓ cup grated Parmesan cheese

1) In a large pasta pot, bring 4 quarts of salted water to a rapid boil. Add the fusilli and cook 8 minutes. Add the peas and carrots and continue to cook until the fusilli is tender but still firm, about 2 minutes longer; drain.

2) Add the soup, garlic, oil, scallions, vinegar, salt, and pepper to the pasta pot. Cook until hot, about 2 minutes.

3) Add the fusilli and Parmesan cheese. Toss thoroughly and serve.

Fusilli with Mexican Salsa

Fresh Mexican salsa, which can be found in most supermarkets in a refrigerated case, either with the produce or near the tortillas in the dairy case, is especially tasty in this dish. But canned or bottled is fine, too. Choose medium or hot, depending on your own preference.

Makes 4 servings

1 pound fusilli
1 tablespoon butter
1 tablespoon oil
1 garlic clove, minced
⅓ cup coarsely chopped cilantro

1 cup salsa
⅓ cup shredded Monterey jack cheese
1 tablespoon grated Romano cheese

1) In a large pasta pot, bring 4 quarts of salted water to a rapid boil. Add the fusilli and cook until tender but still firm, 8 to 12 minutes. Drain in a colander.

2) In the pasta pot, melt the butter in the oil over medium heat. Add the garlic and cook for 1 minute. Return the fusilli to the pot and toss until it is hot and well coated, about 30 seconds. Add the cilantro, salsa, Monterey jack, and Romano cheese.

3) Remove from the heat and stir until well blended. Season with additional salt and pepper to taste. Serve immediately in warm bowls.

Pesto Gnocchi with Vegetables

Gnocchi are Italian *dumplings, often made with potatoes. They are readily available in the freezer section of most supermarkets. Adding vegetables turns this traditional first course into a complete meal. For those of you who are not gnocchi fans, replace the gnocchi with one pound of fusilli.* **Makes 4 to 6 servings**

1½ cups fresh basil leaves
⅓ cup extra-virgin olive oil
3 tablespoons pine nuts or
　walnuts
1 tablespoon butter
2 garlic cloves, minced
¼ teaspoon salt
⅛ teaspoon pepper

⅓ cup grated Parmesan cheese
¼ cup grated Romano cheese
1 pound frozen gnocchi
1½ cups baby carrots
1 cup broccoli florets
1 medium yellow squash, cut into
　¾-inch cubes

1) In a food processor, combine the basil, olive oil, 2 tablespoons of the pine nuts, the butter, garlic, salt, and pepper. Puree until almost smooth. With a rubber spatula, scrape the pesto into a large serving bowl. Stir in the Parmesan and Romano cheeses. Set the pesto aside in a warm place.

2) In a large pasta pot, bring 4 quarts of salted water to a rapid boil. Add the frozen gnocchi and the vegetables. Cook until the gnocchi float to the top, about 6 minutes. Remove 2 tablespoons of the hot pasta water and stir it into the pesto. Immediately drain the gnocchi and vegetables.

3) Add the gnocchi and vegetables to the pesto and toss well to coat. Season with additional salt and pepper to taste. Serve with the remaining pine nuts sprinkled on top.

Penne and Asparagus with Garlic-Tomato Vinaigrette

Makes 4 to 5 servings

1 pound asparagus
1 pound penne
3 tablespoons extra-virgin olive
  oil
5 garlic cloves, minced
¼ cup balsamic vinegar

1 pint of cherry tomatoes, halved
  or quartered if large
½ teaspoon salt
½ teaspoon freshly ground
  pepper
½ cup grated Parmesan cheese

1) Cut the asparagus on the diagonal into the same size lengths as the penne, discarding the tough bottom sections.

2) In a large pasta pot, bring 4 quarts of salted water to a rapid boil. Add the penne and cook 8 minutes. Add the asparagus to the pasta and continue cooking until the penne and asparagus are tender but still firm, 2 to 4 minutes; drain.

3) Add the oil and garlic to the pasta pot. Cook over medium heat, stirring constantly, for 1 minute. Add the vinegar, tomatoes, salt, and pepper. Cook, stirring, just until the tomatoes are slightly warm, about 2 minutes. Pour the garlic-tomato vinaigrette into a small bowl.

4) Return the pasta and asparagus to the pot. Pour the vinaigrette on top and toss well to coat. Add the Parmesan cheese and toss lightly again. Serve warm or at room temperature.

Penne and Broccoli Rabe with Romano Cheese

This is my favorite winter pasta dish. Broccoli rabe, which is in the turnip family, has a distinctive bite that contrasts well with the neutral pasta and salty Romano cheese.   ***Makes 4 servings***

1 pound penne or fusilli
1 bunch of broccoli rabe, tough
  ends removed, cut into
  1-inch pieces
3 tablespoons olive oil
1 tablespoon minced garlic
1 cup chopped fresh plum
  tomatoes or drained canned
  diced tomatoes

¼ to ½ teaspoon crushed hot red
  pepper, to taste
½ teaspoon salt
½ cup grated Romano cheese

1) In a large pasta pot, bring 4 quarts of salted water to a rapid boil. Add the penne and cook 8 minutes. Stir in the broccoli rabe and cook until the penne is tender but still firm, about 2 minutes longer. Drain and transfer to a large serving bowl. Cover to keep warm.

2) To the pasta pot, immediately add the olive oil, garlic, tomatoes, hot pepper, and salt. Cook over high heat, stirring, for 2 minutes.

3) Scrape every drop of the garlic-tomato oil into the large bowl filled with the pasta and broccoli rabe. Toss with ¼ cup of the Romano cheese. Season with additional salt and pepper to taste. Serve, sprinkled with the remaining Romano cheese.

Radiatore with Summer Tomato Sauce

Try this uncooked tomato-basil
*sauce when fresh ripe tomatoes are available. Some American
brands call this radiator-shaped pasta "ruffles." If unavailable, any
short pasta with plenty of nooks and crannies, like fusilli, will work
well.*   ***Makes 4 servings***

2 large beefsteak tomatoes
4 plum tomatoes
⅓ cup extra-virgin olive oil
¼ cup chopped fresh basil
1 large scallion, chopped
1 small garlic clove, minced

¼ teaspoon salt
¼ teaspoon freshly ground
  pepper
1 pound radiatore pasta
Grated Parmesan cheese

1) Halve, seed, and coarsely chop the tomatoes. Add them to a sieve set
over a bowl and press down lightly with a spoon, shaking well to remove
excess juices.

2) In a large serving bowl, mix the tomatoes, olive oil, basil, scallion,
garlic, salt, and pepper.

3) In a large pasta pot, bring 4 quarts of salted water to a rapid boil. Add
the radiatore and cook until tender but still firm, 10 to 12 minutes.
Drain well.

4) Add the radiatore to the tomato sauce. Toss well to coat. Serve
immediately, with a bowl of grated Parmesan cheese on the side.

Ravioli with Lemon-Herb Butter

For an instant meal, frozen *ravioli are boiled for a few minutes with fresh vegetables and then tossed in an aromatic butter. Ready-made ravioli are easily found in the freezer section of most supermarkets.*

Makes 4 to 5 servings

4 tablespoons unsalted butter,
  sliced
2½ tablespoons chopped chives
1 tablespoon plus 1 teaspoon
  fresh lemon juice
¼ teaspoon grated lemon zest
¼ teaspoon dried sage

¼ teaspoon salt
¼ teaspoon freshly ground
  pepper
2 medium carrots, sliced
1 pound frozen cheese ravioli
¾ cup broccoli florets or ½ cup
  fresh or frozen peas

1) In a small glass bowl, microwave the butter on High, covered, until melted, 1 to 2 minutes. Stir in the chives, lemon juice, lemon zest, sage, salt, and pepper. Set the lemon-herb butter aside.

2) Bring a large pasta pot with 4 quarts of salted water to a rapid boil. Add the carrots, ravioli, and broccoli. Cook until the ravioli is just cooked through, 3 to 5 minutes. (It is easiest to tell when the ravioli are done by pulling one out with a slotted spoon, rinsing briefly under cold water, and tasting it.)

3) Drain well and return to the pot or to a serving bowl. Add the lemon-herb butter, toss thoroughly to coat, and serve immediately.

Pasta Shells with Escarole and Chickpeas

The chickpeas play hide-and-seek here with the shells, making this a favorite with children. *A generous grinding of black pepper turns this into a zesty, satisfying dish.* **Makes 4 servings**

1 head of escarole
1 pound small or medium pasta
  shells
1 (14½-ounce) can chickpeas
  (garbanzo beans), rinsed
  and drained
3 tablespoons olive oil

4 garlic cloves, minced
½ teaspoon salt
¾ teaspoon freshly ground
  pepper or 1½ teaspoons
  cracked black pepper
1 tablespoon fresh lemon juice
⅓ cup grated Parmesan cheese

1) Using a large knife, cut the head of escarole crosswise at 1- to 2-inch intervals. Discard the root end, as well as any bruised or damaged leaves. Rinse, but do not dry.

2) Bring 4 quarts of salted water to a rapid boil. Add the pasta shells and cook until they are barely tender but still a little too firm, 8 to 10 minutes. (They will continue to cook for a few minutes while the escarole cooks.) Place the chickpeas in a colander. Drain the pasta on top of the chickpeas to warm them.

3) Working quickly over high heat, add the oil, wet escarole, garlic, salt, and pepper to the pasta pot. Turn the escarole with tongs or a large spoon until it just starts to wilt, about 2 minutes.

4) Return the shells, chickpeas, and 2 tablespoons water to the pot. Cook for 1 to 2 minutes, stirring gently to warm them and distribute the escarole. Stir in the lemon juice and half the cheese. Serve immediately, with the remaining Parmesan cheese sprinkled on top.

Greek Spaghetti

On a hot night in New York, my friend Judy Rabinovitz came up with this quick pasta dinner. A rich, fruity-flavored olive oil works particularly well for this dish, but any olive oil will do. ***Makes 4 servings***

2 tablespoons extra-virgin olive oil
2 medium onions or 1 large Vidalia, chopped
3 garlic cloves, minced
6 plum tomatoes, coarsely chopped
12 large Greek black olives, pitted and chopped

¼ teaspoon salt
¼ teaspoon freshly ground pepper
1 pound spaghetti
½ cup chopped fresh mint
1 cup crumbled feta cheese (about ¼ pound)
2 tablespoons grated Romano cheese

1) In a large pasta pot, heat the olive oil over medium heat. Add the onions and garlic and cook, stirring occasionally, until the onions start to wilt, about 3 minutes. Add the tomatoes, olives, salt, and pepper. Continue to cook, stirring often, until the tomatoes just start to soften a bit, about 2 minutes. Scrape the sauce into a bowl and set aside.

2) Rinse out the pasta pot, fill with 4 quarts water, and bring to a rapid boil. Add the spaghetti and salt to taste. Cook, stirring occasionally, until tender but still firm, 8 to 12 minutes; drain.

3) Immediately return the pasta to the pot. Add the fresh tomato mixture sauce and toss over heat until warm, about 1 minute. Mix in the fresh mint, feta, and Romano cheese. Season with additional salt and pepper to taste. Serve immediately.

Spaghetti with Roasted Peppers and Sun-Dried Tomato Pesto

Dry-pack sun-dried tomatoes *work wonderfully in this dish. They are less expensive than those packed in olive oil and are available in the produce department of most supermarkets. If you want to save time here, substitute jarred roasted red peppers, rinsed and drained, for the bell peppers, in which case, skip step 2.* **Makes 4 servings**

6 sun-dried tomato halves
2 medium red bell peppers
2 garlic cloves, peeled and smashed
3 tablespoons extra-virgin olive oil
1 teaspoon red wine vinegar
Pinch of sugar

1 teaspoon salt
¼ teaspoon freshly ground pepper
1 pound spaghetti
¼ cup grated Parmesan cheese
½ cup walnuts, coarsely chopped,
    preferably toasted

1) Soak sun-dried tomatoes in a small bowl covered with hot water until soft, about 15 minutes.

2) Meanwhile, roast the peppers directly over a gas flame or under a broiler as close to the heat as possible, turning, until they are charred, about 10 minutes. Place in a brown paper bag or cover with a kitchen towel and let stand until they are cool enough to handle. Remove the stems and seeds. Then with your hands or a knife, remove the skins. Don't worry if there are some charred bits left.

3) In a food processor, combine the sun-dried tomatoes, roasted peppers, garlic, olive oil, vinegar, sugar, salt, pepper, and 2 tablespoons water. Puree until smooth. Set the pesto aside.

4) In a large pasta pot, bring 4 quarts of salted water to a rapid boil. Add the spaghetti, bending it gently with a wooden spoon once it is in the pot to fit it all in. Cook, stirring occasionally, until tender but still firm, 8 to 12 minutes; drain. In the pasta pot or a serving bowl, toss the hot pasta with the Parmesan cheese, sun-dried tomato pesto, and nuts. Serve at once.

Spaghettini with Fennel, Currants, and Pine Nuts

The gentle anise-flavored *fennel is added both cooked and raw to this subtle dish.*

Makes 4 servings

1 medium fennel bulb
1 pound spaghettini
3 tablespoons olive oil
3 garlic cloves, minced
¼ teaspoon crushed hot red
    pepper

¼ teaspoon fennel seeds
¼ cup pine nuts
¼ cup currants
½ teaspoon salt

1) Remove the outer stalks from the fennel bulb and discard. Trim off the fennel tops and chop 2 tablespoons of the green fronds if they are attached. Cut the fennel bulb lengthwise in half and chop finely. Set both aside.

2) In a large pasta pot, bring 4 quarts of salted water to a rapid boil. Add the spaghettini, bending it gently with a wooden spoon once it is in the pot to fit it all in. Cook, stirring occasionally, until tender but still firm, about 8 minutes; drain.

3) Add the oil, garlic, hot pepper, and fennel seeds to the pasta pot. Cook over medium-high heat until the garlic smells fragrant, 1 to 2 minutes. Add about two-thirds of the chopped fennel bulb, the pine nuts, currants, and salt. Cook, stirring continuously, until the fennel softens slightly, about 3 minutes.

4) Return the pasta to the pot. Add the remaining chopped fennel bulb and toss until the pasta is warm, about 1 minute. Serve in bowls with the fennel greens sprinkled on top.

Summary Tortellini Salad

his pasta salad has become an American summer staple because it is easy to assemble, pretty, and a surefire crowd pleaser. If you choose to serve the salad cold, be sure to taste for seasoning; it may need a little more salt, pepper, and vinegar after chilling. ***Makes 4 servings***

2 tablespoons plus 1 teaspoon red wine vinegar
1 tablespoon grainy mustard
1 garlic clove, minced
½ teaspoon salt
¼ teaspoon freshly ground pepper
2 tablespoons olive oil
2 tablespoons chopped fresh basil or parsley

2 small scallions, sliced
18 ounces cheese tortellini, preferably spinach (green)
2 small carrots, peeled and thinly sliced
6 Calamata or Greek olives, pitted and sliced
1 yellow bell pepper, diced
3 tablespoons grated Parmesan cheese

1) In a small bowl, combine 2 tablespoons of the vinegar with the mustard, garlic, salt, and pepper. With a fork or whisk, slowly beat in the olive oil. Stir in the basil and scallions. Set the dressing aside.

2) In a large pasta pot, bring 4 quarts of salted water to a rapid boil. Add the tortellini and cook until just tender, about 5 minutes, adding the carrots during the last minute of cooking. Drain and rinse briefly under cold running water; shake the colander to remove excess water.

3) In a medium bowl, toss the tortellini with the dressing, olives, and yellow pepper. Serve at room temperature or cover and refrigerate until chilled. Sprinkle the Parmesan cheese on top just before serving.

Vermicelli with Cilantro Pesto

½ cup slivered almonds
2 small bunches or 1 large bunch
  of cilantro
2 garlic cloves, minced
¼ cup olive oil

¾ teaspoon salt
¼ teaspoon cayenne
½ cup grated Romano cheese
1 pound vermicelli or linguine

1) In a dry pasta pot, toast the almonds over medium heat, stirring constantly to prevent burning. They are done when they smell aromatic and nutty and just start to color, about 3 to 5 minutes. Place ¼ cup in the food processor; set aside the remaining ¼ cup.

2) Cut most of the stems off the cilantro and rinse well. Tear to fit into a cup measure; you should have 1¼ cups tightly packed, mostly leaves.

3) Add the cilantro, garlic, olive oil, salt, cayenne, and ¼ cup water to the almonds in the food processor. Puree until smooth but not completely pureed. Using a rubber spatula, scrape the cilantro pesto into a large serving bowl and stir in the cheese.

4) In a large pasta pot, bring 4 quarts of salted water to a rapid boil. Add the vermicelli, bending it gently with a wooden spoon once it is in the pot to fit it all in. Cook, stirring occasionally, until tender but still firm, about 10 minutes. Drain and immediately add the pasta to the cilantro pesto in the serving bowl. Toss to mix well. Serve with the remaining toasted almonds sprinkled on top.

Go-West Wagon Wheels with Smoky Tomato Sauce

Chipotle chiles add a unique smoky flavor as well as fiery heat to this simple chunky tomato sauce. They are sold dried or canned in adobo sauce in many supermarkets and specialty food stores. ***Makes 4 to 6 servings***

3 medium dried chipotle peppers
   or 2 teaspoons canned
   chipotle peppers
   or ½ teaspoon cayenne
2 tablespoons vegetable oil
1 medium onion, chopped
1 medium green bell pepper,
   chopped
1 medium carrot, chopped

1 medium celery rib, chopped
3 garlic cloves, minced
2 (14½-ounce) cans diced peeled
   tomatoes, juices reserved
¼ cup tomato paste
1 teaspoon salt
1 pound rotelle wagon wheel pasta
½ cup shredded Monterey jack
   cheese

1) If you are using dried chipotle chiles, set them in a small bowl covered with hot water until they soften, about 20 minutes. Remove the stems and seeds; chop the chiles. If using canned, mince them.

2) In a pasta pot, heat the oil over medium heat. Add the onion, bell pepper, carrot, celery, and garlic. Cook, stirring occasionally, until the onion is softened and translucent, about 5 minutes.

3) Add the tomatoes with their juices, tomato paste, chipotle chiles, and salt. Cook for about 10 minutes, stirring occasionally, until the sauce thickens and tastes slightly smoky. With a rubber spatula, scrape the sauce into a medium bowl and set aside.

4) Rinse out the pasta pot and fill with 4 quarts of salted water. Bring to a rapid boil over high heat. Add the wagon wheels and cook, stirring occasionally, until tender but still firm, 10 to 12 minutes; drain. Return the sauce to the pot, add the cooked pasta, and toss well until warm, about 30 seconds. Serve in bowls with the cheese sprinkled on top.

Szechuan Cold Sesame Noodles

This quick summer favorite
uses dried noodles, sometimes labeled "Chinese Plain
Noodles," located in the Asian section of the supermarket.

Makes 4 to 5 servings

¼ cup chunky peanut butter
¼ cup balsamic vinegar
2 tablespoons soy sauce
2 tablespoons Asian sesame oil
1 teaspoon vegetable oil
½ to 1 teaspoon hot chili oil, or
   more to taste

2 teaspoons sugar
1 garlic clove, minced
1 (8-ounce) package dried
   Chinese noodles
2 medium carrots, shredded
2 scallions, thinly sliced on the
   diagonal

1) In a large bowl, whisk together the peanut butter with 3 tablespoons
hot water until well blended. Gradually whisk in the vinegar, soy sauce,
sesame oil, vegetable oil, hot oil, sugar, and garlic.

2) In a small pasta pot or large saucepan, bring 3 quarts of lightly salted
water to a rapid boil. Add the noodles to the pot. Cook, stirring
occasionally to break them up, until tender but still firm, about 5 minutes.
Drain and rinse briefly under cold water.

3) Add the pasta to the sauce in the bowl and toss well to coat. Serve
each portion on a plate and top with the carrots and scallions.

Teriyaki Tofu on Buckwheat Noodles with Watercress

Buckwheat noodles, called *soba, can be found in health food stores, in Asian markets, and in some supermarkets. This dish is good either hot or at room temperature. Sake is a Japanese rice wine. It is lovely served warm in small cups with this dish.* ***Makes 3 to 4 servings***

1 (14-ounce) container extra-firm or firm tofu
⅓ cup sake or dry white wine
⅓ cup tamari or soy sauce
2 tablespoons confectioners' sugar
1 tablespoon Asian sesame oil
1 teaspoon minced fresh ginger

¼ teaspoon cayenne
6 ounces buckwheat noodles
3 scallions, thinly sliced
2 medium bunches of watercress, tough stems removed
1 tablespoon sesame seeds

1) Drain the tofu well. If you have time, to remove the excess liquid: Place the tofu on a plate, top with another plate, weight with a heavy can or skillet, and let drain about 20 minutes. Cut into ½-inch cubes.

2) In a small bowl, whisk together the sake, tamari, sugar, sesame oil, ginger, and cayenne. Set this teriyaki sauce aside.

3) In a large pasta pot, bring 4 quarts of lightly salted water to a rapid boil. Add the buckwheat noodles and cook, stirring occasionally, until tender but still firm, about 7 minutes. Drain the noodles.

4) Working quickly, add the reserved teriyaki sauce to the pot. Bring the sauce a boil over medium-high heat. Immediately add the scallions, watercress, and tofu. With tongs or a wooden spoon, stir gently until the watercress is wilted and the tofu is warmed through, about 3 minutes.

5) Return the buckwheat noodles to the pot and stir gently with tongs to mix. If you are serving the noodles at room temperature, they may be served now. But if you are serving them hot, stir until the noodles are warm, about 2 minutes. Serve in bowls, topped with a sprinkling of sesame seeds.

Vegetables in the Wok

Americans have
*embraced the wok as a common kitchen utensil
for over two decades. And with good reason: It is a
fast way to cook healthy foods that look and taste
great. Stir-frying uses a minimum of oil. And in the
wok over high heat, vegetables cook up tender-
crisp, colorful, and packed with flavor.*

*In this chapter, the tremendous versatility of the
utensil is maximized to produce a wide variety of
dishes, from the traditional Chinese Buddha's De-
light to a down-home vegetarian version of Quick
Bean Picadillo and an Italian-inspired Wilted Greens
with Gorgonzola Croutons.*

*The wok is an ideal roomy place to cook piles of
leafy greens or vegetables that need lots of space,*

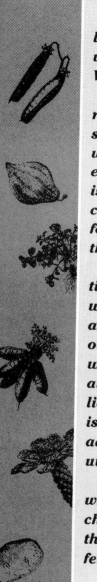

like the bulky cabbage in Sweet and Sour Cabbage with Potatoes and Raisins or the spinach in Wokked Noodles with Spinach and Mushrooms.

Wok cooking techniques are simple, fast, and direct. The food is cut and assembled beforehand, stir-fried quickly, and eaten immediately. This makes wok cooking practical for both entertaining and everyday cooking. But be prepared. The cooking time is so short that it is best to have all your food, including your seasonings, by the side of the stove before you turn on the heat. Once the cooking begins, there won't be any time to rummage around.

Generally wok cooking starts with hot oil. Sometimes aromatics like ginger or scallion are cooked with the oil to flavor it first. The vegetables are added and "stir-fried," that is, moved around rapidly over high heat. Next, some form of liquid—broth, wine, soy sauce, or chopped tomatoes—is generally added to the wok. Sometimes, to finish a dish, the liquid is thickened, often with cornstarch, which is mixed with a liquid, like water or broth, then added to the hot wok. It thickens quickly as the liquid boils. In just a few minutes, dinner is on the table.

There are a number of woks on the market, any of which is perfectly adequate for the recipes in this chapter. But if you are thinking of buying a wok for the first time or replacing an old wok, here are a few helpful tips. Woks are designed for cooking over

ONE-POT VEGETARIAN DISHES

a high flame. For the home kitchen, especially those with electric stoves, a flat-bottomed wok can be quite useful, because it brings the food to be cooked closer to the heat source. Flat bottoms also increase the stability of the wok. Classic woks with a rounded bottom often come with a metal ring; these are often not needed on a gas stove, where the frame around the burner can act as a stand.

While you stir-fry, one hand should be holding the wok still. Look for a wok with a stay-cool handle, like wood, that you can grip firmly when cooking. Or use a kitchen mitt on the hand holding the wok. For a cover, anything works that doesn't allow too much steam to escape. To stir the vegetables, use a rounded spatula or a large, long-handled spoon.

A traditional wok is easy to clean. While it is still warm, rinse it immediately with hot water, cleaning it with an unsoaped sponge. Wipe or shake it dry. Then, while you are enjoying your stir-fried supper, sit it on the still warm burner. Before you put it away, turn on the burner to evaporate any remaining water, then wipe it very lightly with vegetable oil to maintain the finish and develop a slick, seasoned coating. As an alternative to the traditional wok, some people enjoy the new nonstick woks. I've called for nonstick whenever I've used a bare minimum of oil. If your regular wok is very well seasoned, it should serve as well.

Wilted Greens with Gorgonzola Croutons

Warm salads make popular light meals. The wok is a useful tool for cooking greens, as they take up a lot of room before they wilt. This Italian-inspired dish makes a lovely lunch or casual supper. **Makes 4 servings**

10 ounces fresh spinach leaves, stems removed
1 large head of escarole
2 ounces Gorgonzola cheese, at room temperature
2 ounces cream cheese, at room temperature

8 to 12 slices of Italian, French, or peasant bread
¼ cup olive oil
4 garlic cloves, thinly sliced
½ teaspoon salt
1½ tablespoons red wine vinegar
½ small red onion, sliced

1) Cut or tear the spinach leaves crosswise into 2 or 3 pieces. Slice the whole head of escarole crosswise into 4 or 5 pieces, starting at the ends of the leaves and discarding the root end. Rinse the greens well; drain.

2) In a small bowl, mash together the Gorgonzola and cream cheeses with a spoon until well blended. In a toaster oven or preheated 400 degree F oven, toast the bread until warm, 3 to 5 minutes. With a butter knife, spread a little cheese on each warm bread slice. Hold the Gorgonzola croutons in a warm place.

3) In a wok, heat the oil over medium-high heat. Add the garlic and enough greens to fill the wok about three-fourths of the way up. Cook, turning the greens with tongs until they wilt a bit, about 2 minutes. Add the salt and more greens. Repeat until all the greens can just fit into the wok, 3 to 5 minutes total. Sprinkle the vinegar over the greens, cover, and cook for 1 minute. Uncover and toss with the tongs until the greens are wilted but some of the escarole is still crunchy, 30 to 60 seconds.

4) With the tongs, transfer the greens onto plates or a large platter. Sprinkle with the red onion slices and top with the Gorgonzola croutons.

Quick Bean Picadillo

My students were skeptical when I handed them this recipe, but they adored it both warm and cold. Despite the long list of ingredients, this dish is a snap to throw together. Just assemble everything by the side of the stove, as the dish cooks quickly. Serve alone or with rice or corn bread. If you plan on serving this dish at room temperature or cold, simply add a tablespoon of vinegar. **Makes 6 servings**

¼ cup sliced almonds
3 tablespoons vegetable oil
1 large onion, chopped
2 jalapeño peppers, seeded and
  finely chopped
1 celery rib, diced
2 teaspoons ground cumin
2 teaspoons ground coriander
1 teaspoon dried oregano
½ teaspoon cinnamon
Pinch of ground cloves
1 (28-ounce) can plum tomatoes,
  drained

3 garlic cloves, chopped
½ cup chopped green olives,
  with or without pimientos
2 (19-ounce) cans kidney beans,
  rinsed and drained
1½ cups fresh corn kernels or
  1 (10-ounce) package frozen
  corn, thawed
½ cup raisins
3 tablespoons white wine vinegar
  or cider vinegar
½ teaspoon salt

1) In a dry wok, toast the almonds over medium heat, stirring constantly, until they are lightly toasted, golden, and smell lightly of almonds, 2 to 3 minutes; do not brown. Remove from the wok and set aside.

2) Increase the heat to medium-high. Add the oil and then the onion, jalapeño peppers, celery, cumin, coriander, oregano, cinnamon, and cloves. Cook, stirring constantly for 1 minute to combine the flavors.

3) Add the tomatoes and stir, breaking them up with a wooden spoon. Add the garlic, olives, beans, corn, raisins, vinegar, and salt. Reduce the heat to medium, cover, and simmer 10 minutes. Ladle into warm bowls. Sprinkle the toasted almonds on top.

Bok Choy and Browned Onions with Broken Noodles

This subtle, surprisingly
*attractive dish is even better cold the next day. It uses a package
of ramen noodles, found in the Asian foods section of most
supermarkets.*

Makes 4 servings

1 (14½-ounce) can vegetable
  broth
1 tablespoon cornstarch
1½ tablespoons vegetable oil
2 teaspoons butter
2 nickel-sized slices of fresh ginger
1 large Vidalia onion or small
  Spanish onion, sliced
2 carrots, thinly sliced
1 large red bell pepper, cut into
  1-inch cubes

1 small bok choy, cut into 1-inch
  pieces (about 4 cups), white
  stems and green leaves
  separated
1 (3-ounce) package ramen
  noodles, without the
  seasoning packet
1½ tablespoons soy sauce
1 tablespoon fresh lemon juice

1) In a small bowl, combine ⅓ cup stock with the cornstarch. Set aside.

2) In a wok, heat the oil over medium-high heat for 1 minute. Add the
butter. As soon as it melts, add the ginger, onion, carrots, and red pepper.
Cook, stirring constantly, until the onion turns light brown, about 3 minutes.

3) Add the whites of the bok choy. Stir-fry for 2 minutes. Using your
hands, break the noodles into small pieces right into the wok. Add the
remaining broth, the soy sauce, 3 tablespoons water, and the bok choy
greens, pushing all the noodles down into the liquid. Cook, stirring
occasionally, until the noodles are tender, 3 to 5 minutes.

4) Stir the cornstarch and stock to blend thoroughly. Turn the heat up
to high and drizzle it over the top of the vegetables. Toss thoroughly until
the liquid boils and becomes a bit thickened, 1 to 2 minutes. Add the lemon
juice and serve immediately.

Broccoli Stir-Fry with Black Bean Sauce

This intensely flavored dish is terrific with plain white rice. Fresh apricots, melon, or oranges finish the meal perfectly. **Makes 3 to 4 servings**

2 tablespoons fermented black beans
2 tablespoons apricot or peach jam
1 large garlic clove, peeled
1 thin slice of fresh ginger
2 teaspoons Szechuan hot sauce
2 large scallions, cut into 1-inch lengths, white and green separated

2 tablespoons vegetable oil
1 large head of broccoli, cut into 1-inch florets
1 large red bell pepper, diced
1 tablespoon cornstarch
1 teaspoon Asian sesame oil

1) In a food processor, combine the black beans, jam, garlic, ginger, and hot sauce. Pulse until the garlic and ginger are finely chopped.

2) In a wok, cook the scallion whites in the oil over high heat for 1 minute. Carefully add the broccoli and red pepper; the oil may splatter a bit. Cook, stirring frequently, until the broccoli turns bright green, about 2 minutes. With a rubber spatula, scrape the black bean sauce into the wok. Stir to coat the vegetables, then add ⅓ cup water. Cover and cook until the broccoli is tender but still firm, about 3 minutes.

3) Meanwhile, in a small bowl, combine the cornstarch with 3 tablespoons water. Stir until smooth and blended. When the broccoli is ready to serve, uncover the wok and stir in the cornstarch mixture and scallion greens. Bring to a boil, stirring until thickened and the vegetables are evenly coated with sauce, 1 to 2 minutes. Stir in the sesame oil and serve immediately.

Buddha's Delight

This medley of brightly colored vegetables may be served alone or with rice.

Makes 4 servings

1 cup canned vegetable stock
1½ tablespoons apricot
  preserves or 1 teaspoon
  sugar
1½ tablespoons cornstarch
1 tablespoon dry sherry
1 tablespoon soy sauce
2 tablespoons vegetable oil
3 large leeks (white and tender
  green), well rinsed and cut
  into ½-inch pieces
2 thin slices of fresh ginger
2 medium carrots, sliced

1 pound asparagus, tough ends
  removed, cut into 1½-inch
  pieces
1 medium red bell pepper, cut
  into thin strips
¼ teaspoon crushed hot red
  pepper
¼ teaspoon salt
1 (14-ounce) can baby corn,
  drained and cut in half if large
1 (8-ounce) can sliced water
  chestnuts
2 teaspoons Asian sesame oil

1) In a small bowl, blend the stock, apricot preserves, cornstarch, sherry, and soy sauce. Set the sauce aside.

2) In a wok, heat the oil over high heat for 1 minute. Add the leeks, ginger, and carrots. Cook, stirring constantly, for 1 minute.

3) Add the asparagus, bell pepper, hot pepper, and salt. Cook, stirring occasionally, until the asparagus are half cooked, 2 to 3 minutes. Add the baby corn and water chestnuts and cook, stirring, until warm, about 2 minutes.

4) Stir the reserved sauce and pour over the vegetables. Bring to a boil, stirring occasionally, until thickened, 2 to 3 minutes. Remove from the heat and stir in the sesame oil. Serve at once.

Bulgur Succotash

This is a whole-grain version
of a traditional American vegetable dish. Despite the long list
of ingredients, it is a snap to pull together. ***Makes 4 servings***

3 tablespoons olive oil
1 small red onion, chopped
1 teaspoon paprika
1 teaspoon ground coriander
½ teaspoon ground cumin
½ teaspoon fennel seeds
1 teaspoon salt
1 (10-ounce) package frozen
   baby lima beans

1 cup fresh or frozen corn
   kernels
1 cup bulgur
1 large tomato, chopped
⅓ cup chopped cilantro
¼ to ½ teaspoon cayenne, to
   taste
1 lemon, cut into wedges

1) In a wok, heat the oil over medium heat. Add the onion, paprika,
coriander, cumin, fennel, and salt. Cook, stirring often, until the onion is
soft and the spices smell aromatic, 3 to 5 minutes.

2) Add the lima beans, corn, bulgur, tomato, and 1⅓ cups hot tap water.
Bring to a boil, reduce the heat to medium, cover, and cook, stirring
occasionally, until almost all the liquid is absorbed, about 15 minutes.

3) Stir in the cilantro and season with cayenne to taste. Accompany with
lemon wedges.

Sweet and Sour Cabbage with Potatoes and Raisins

*C*hewy sourdough or peasant
bread makes a good accompaniment for this dish. Savoy
cabbage has a slightly more delicate taste and texture than
ordinary cabbage, but if it is unavailable, use any green
cabbage. If you enjoy extra richness, pass a bowl of dilled sour
cream on the side.   ***Makes 4 servings***

2 medium red potatoes, peeled
   and cut into 6 wedges each
3 tablespoons olive oil
1 large red onion, sliced
1 medium Savoy cabbage, root
   end discarded, sliced
½ cup raisins

1 teaspoon salt
¾ teaspoon caraway seeds
⅛ teaspoon freshly ground
   pepper
3 tablespoons red wine vinegar
1 tablespoon sugar
2 medium carrots, shredded

1) In a wok, bring 6 cups salted water to a boil over high heat. Add the
potatoes and cook until tender, about 15 minutes. Drain and return to
the wok to heat until dry. Set the potatoes aside.

2) Add the oil and heat over medium-high heat. Add the onion and
cook, stirring, until it just starts to wilt, 1 to 2 minutes. Add the cabbage,
breaking it apart with your hands as you add it to the wok and turning it with
tongs to coat evenly with oil, about 1 minute.

3) Add the raisins, salt, caraway, and pepper. Continue to cook, stirring
frequently with tongs, until the cabbage just starts to wilt, about
5 minutes. Add the vinegar, sugar, and carrots. Continue to cook, stirring
occasionally, until the cabbage is wilted but some of it is still crispy,
about 5 minutes longer.

4) Return the potatoes to the wok, reduce the heat to medium, cover
and cook, tossing once or twice, until heated through, 2 to 3 minutes.
Serve hot or at room temperature.

Green Bean Stir-Fry

If unavailable, Jerusalem artichokes may be replaced by one half cup diced jicama or a can of drained, sliced water chestnuts. Serve alone or over rice.

Makes 4 servings

3 large dried shiitake
   mushrooms
1 cup boiling water
1 tablespoon cornstarch
1 tablespoon soy sauce
1 tablespoon sherry
1 teaspoon sugar
1 garlic clove, minced
2½ tablespoons vegetable oil
1 large jalapeño pepper, seeded
   and minced

4 scallions, cut into 1-inch
   pieces, white and green
   separated
1 teaspoon minced fresh ginger
1 pound green beans, ends
   removed
1 large carrot, sliced
½ teaspoon salt
3 large Jerusalem artichokes,
   peeled and sliced

1) In a small heatproof bowl, cover the dried shiitakes with the boiling water; let stand until softened, about 15 minutes. Remove the mushrooms, cut off and discard the stems, and chop and reserve the caps. Strain the soaking liquid and reserve in a small bowl. Add the cornstarch, soy, sherry, sugar, and garlic to the soaking liquid. Stir to mix well. Set this sauce aside.

2) In a wok, heat the oil over high heat. Add the jalapeño, scallion whites, and ginger and cook, stirring, for 1 minute. Add the green beans, carrot, and salt. Cook, stirring occasionally, until the beans are tender, 5 to 10 minutes.

3) Add the shiitake mushrooms, Jerusalem artichokes, and scallion greens to the wok. Cook, stirring constantly, until the vegetables are hot and the scallions are wilted, 2 to 3 minutes.

4) Mix the reserved sauce well, then, with a rubber spatula, scrape every bit over the vegetables. Don't stir until the liquid starts to boil, about 2 minutes; then stir until the vegetables are coated and the sauce has thickened, 1 to 2 minutes. Serve immediately.

Crispy Maifun Noodle Salad

This pretty, festive salad is a
unique celebration of color and texture—the perfect party dish.
The only cooked component of this salad is the maifun, a thin type
of cellophane noodle, which may be found in the Asian section
of many supermarkets.

Don't be put off by the amount of oil called for; the noodles don't
absorb much. The leftover oil is drained off and reserved for
future use. Chinese five-spice powder is available in the spice
section of some supermarkets and in all Asian food stores, but
it can be omitted.

For a spectacular presentation, the remaining half package of
noodles can be fried in some of the remaining oil and used to
surround the entire salad. **Makes 4 to 6 servings**

1 teaspoon Szechuan
  peppercorns or ¼ teaspoon
  crushed hot red pepper
3 tablespoons rice vinegar
1 teaspoon salt
2 garlic cloves, minced
½ teaspoon Chinese five-spice
  powder
2 tablespoons sugar
¼ teaspoon minced fresh ginger
1 cup plus 3 tablespoons
  vegetable oil

1 tablespoon Asian sesame oil
½ package maifun (rice stick)
  noodles (3 ounces)
½ head of iceberg lettuce, shredded
4 medium scallions, greens only,
  thinly sliced on the diagonal
1 red bell pepper, cut into thin
  strips
¼ pound snow peas, cut into
  thin strips
2 tablespoons chopped peanuts
1 tablespoon sesame seeds

1) Toast the Szechuan peppercorns in a dry wok over medium heat,
stirring constantly, for 1 minute, or until they smell fragrant. Remove
and grind in an empty pepper mill, spice grinder, or with a mortar and
pestle. If you are using crushed hot red pepper, omit this step.

2) In a small bowl, combine the Szechuan peppercorns, vinegar, salt, garlic, five-spice powder, sugar, and ginger. Slowly whisk in 3 tablespoons vegetable oil and the sesame oil. Set this dressing aside.

3) With scissors, cut the noodles into 3-inch pieces. Heat the remaining oil in the wok over high heat until very hot, about 3 minutes. Test the temperature by tossing a small piece of noodle into the oil. It should puff up immediately. Cook the noodles in 3 or 4 batches by dropping each batch into the oil and turning the noodles with tongs until you see that they are all thoroughly cooked. They should be white and not transparent, about 1 minute. Remove each batch to a paper towel to drain.

4) In a large bowl, toss the cooked noodles, lettuce, and scallions with about three-fourths of the reserved dressing. Pile the salad high onto individual plates or onto a platter. In the same bowl, toss the red pepper and snow peas in the remaining dressing. Heap the vegetables in the center of the salads or salad, and top with the peanuts and sesame seeds. Serve immediately.

Wokked Noodles with Spinach and Mushrooms

Ramen noodles are a boon *for the busy cook, as they cook swiftly and have a satisfying texture. To ease preparation time, packages of sliced mushrooms and washed spinach are available in some supermarkets.*

Makes 4 to 5 servings

1½ teaspoons salt
2 packages ramen noodles, without the seasoning packet
2 tablespoons vegetable oil
1 medium red onion, thinly sliced
¼ pound fresh shiitake mushrooms, stems removed, caps sliced
8 ounces white button mushrooms, sliced

½ teaspoon dried thyme leaves
1 (10-ounce) package fresh spinach, stems removed
¼ cup flour
1½ cups milk
½ teaspoon grated nutmeg
½ teaspoon freshly ground pepper
½ cup shredded Gruyère or Swiss cheese

1) In a wok, bring 4 cups of water to a rapid boil. Add ½ teaspoon salt and the noodles. Using tongs, break up the noodles and cook just until softened, 1 to 2 minutes. Drain in a colander and rinse under cold water.

2) Dry the wok and heat the oil over medium-high heat. Add the red onion and cook until it starts to brown, 3 to 5 minutes. Add the shiitakes, white mushrooms, and thyme and cook, stirring frequently, until the mushrooms are soft, about 5 minutes. Tear the spinach with your hands as you add it to the wok, stirring often, until it wilts, 3 to 5 minutes.

3) Reduce the heat to medium. Sprinkle the remaining 1 teaspoon salt and the flour evenly over the spinach-mushroom mixture, stirring constantly and scraping the bottom of the wok to prevent sticking.

4) Pour in the milk. Cook over high heat until it has thickened into a light sauce, about 2 minutes. Add the noodles, nutmeg, and pepper, stirring, until the dish is hot. Serve in bowls, sprinkled with the cheese.

Mushroom Braised Tofu with Snow Peas

In this dish, soft clouds of tofu are sauced with savory mushrooms. Snow peas add green color, flavor, and crunch. Serve in bowls alone or over rice. To save time, purchase sliced fresh mushrooms or slice them in a food processor. ***Makes 4 servings***

7 large dried shiitake
  mushrooms
¾ cup boiling water
1 (16-ounce) container soft tofu
2 tablespoons vegetable oil
2 slices of fresh ginger
4 scallions, sliced, white and
  green separated
⅛ teaspoon crushed hot red
  pepper

8 ounces fresh white button
  mushrooms, sliced
¼ teaspoon salt
1 tablespoon soy sauce
1 tablespoon dry sherry
1 teaspoon sugar
¼ pound snow peas, strings
  removed, cut into lengthwise
  thirds

1) In a medium heatproof bowl, cover the dried mushrooms with the boiling water; let stand until softened, about 15 minutes. Cut off and discard the stems. Slice the mushroom caps. Strain the soaking liquid through a paper towel–lined sieve or a coffee filter, reserving the liquid. Drain the tofu. Cut it lengthwise into 4 slices, then cut each piece into 4 pieces.

2) In a wok, heat the oil over high heat. Stir in the ginger, scallion whites, and hot pepper. Add the shiitake and fresh mushrooms and salt and cook, stirring frequently, until the mushrooms are tender and aromatic, 3 to 5 minutes.

3) Stir in the soy sauce, sherry, and sugar. Reduce the heat to medium. Carefully set the tofu pieces on top of the mushrooms; add the reserved soaking liquid. Cover and cook until the tofu is hot and the sauce is bubbling, about 5 minutes. Scatter the scallion greens and snow peas on top, cover, and steam for 1 minute. Serve immediately.

Lemon-Soy Quinoa Stir-Fry

High-protein quinoa is a quick-cooking grain, available in some supermarkets and in all health food stores. In this colorful stir-fry, quinoa's earthy taste complements the robust flavor of brussels sprouts.

Makes 3 servings

1½ tablespoons vegetable oil
1 cup quinoa
1 teaspoon salt
⅛ teaspoon pepper
1 medium onion, sliced
1 pound brussels sprouts, root
    ends trimmed, halved

1 basket cherry tomatoes, cut in
    half
2 tablespoons fresh lemon juice
2 tablespoons soy sauce
2 teaspoons sugar
3 tablespoons dry-roasted
    sunflower seeds

1) Brush a wok with about 1½ teaspoons vegetable oil. Add 1¾ cups water and bring to a boil. Add the quinoa, ½ teaspoon salt, and the pepper. Reduce the heat to medium, cover, and cook until all the liquid is absorbed, about 15 minutes. Remove the quinoa from the wok and set aside.

2) In the same wok, heat the remaining 1 tablespoon oil over medium-high heat. Add the onion, brussels sprouts, 2 tablespoons water, and the remaining ½ teaspoon salt. Cook, stirring frequently, until the sprouts are bright green and the onion starts to brown, about 5 minutes.

3) Add the cherry tomatoes, lemon juice, soy sauce, and sugar. Cook, stirring gently, until the tomatoes are warmed through but still hold their shape, about 2 minutes. Return the quinoa to the wok and stir gently to combine. Serve in individual bowls, with the sunflower seeds sprinkled on top.

Santa Fe Stir-Fry with Squash, Sweet Peppers, and Corn

Canned *mild green chiles can be found in the Mexican section of supermarkets.*

Makes 4 servings

2 tablespoons olive oil
1 large onion, sliced
1 large green bell pepper, sliced
1 large red bell pepper, sliced
1 large yellow bell pepper, sliced
1 medium zucchini or yellow
   squash, sliced
1¼ teaspoons ground cumin
½ teaspoon salt

1¼ cups fresh or frozen corn
   kernels
1 (4-ounce) can chopped mild
   green chiles, drained
2 tablespoons vegetable broth
   or water
1 cup shredded Monterey jack
   cheese

1) In a wok, heat the oil over medium-high heat. Add the onion, bell peppers, zucchini, cumin, and salt. Cook, stirring frequently, until the vegetables are wilted but still firm, 5 to 7 minutes.

2) Add the corn, chiles, and broth. Cook, stirring frequently, until the corn is tender and hot, 2 to 3 minutes. Serve in bowls, topped with the cheese.

Battered Vegetables with Lime

This is the only fried dish in the book, and it is totally satisfying in its simplicity. Lightly battered vegetables are fried in a wok. While piping hot, they are sprinkled with kosher salt and freshly ground pepper and served with a wedge of lime. The effect is not unlike tempura. Fried food is best served immediately, but it can be held in a 200 degree F oven on a platter lined with a paper towel for draining.

Makes 4 to 6 servings

1 large yam, peeled and thinly sliced

1 medium zucchini, cut into thin slices

1 (8-ounce) package small mushrooms, wiped clean, stems removed

1 green or red bell pepper, sliced into 1-inch strips

1 small head of broccoli, cut into 1-inch florets with no stem

1⅓ cups flour

3 cups vegetable oil

1 teaspoon kosher salt

¼ teaspoon freshly ground pepper

1 large lime, cut into wedges

1) Prepare all the vegetables and set them on a platter next to the stove. Have a second platter lined with a paper towel ready by the side of the stove for the fried vegetables. Pour 1⅓ cups cold water into a medium bowl. Slowly whisk in the flour until smooth.

2) Heat the oil in a wok over high heat until it reaches 360 degrees F. If you don't have a deep-fry thermometer, drop a little batter into the oil. It should drop to the bottom, quickly float up to the top again, and puff.

3) In batches of about 6, dip the vegetables into the batter, letting the excess batter drip off, and then drop them quickly into the hot oil, one at a time. Turn them occasionally with tongs, until an ivory-colored crust is formed all around each vegetable, about 3 minutes. Remove to drain on the paper towels. Serve immediately, sprinkled with the salt and pepper and accompanied by lime wedges.

Lemon-Soy Vegetable Stir-Fry

This colorful stir-fry of brussels sprouts and cherry tomatoes can be tossed together in minutes. Serve with a wedge of peasant bread.   ***Makes 2 to 3 servings***

1 tablespoon vegetable oil
1 medium onion, sliced
1 pound brussels sprouts, root
   ends trimmed, halved
½ teaspoon salt
1 pint cherry tomatoes, cut in
   half

2 tablespoons fresh lemon juice
2 tablespoons soy sauce
2 teaspoons sugar
3 tablespoons dry-roasted
   sunflower seeds

1) In a wok, heat the oil over medium-high heat. Add the onion, brussels sprouts, 1 tablespoon water, and the salt. Cook, stirring frequently, until the sprouts are bright green and the onion starts to brown, about 5 minutes.

2) Add the cherry tomatoes, lemon juice, soy sauce, and sugar. Cook, stirring gently, until the tomatoes are warmed through but not mushy, about 2 minutes. Serve in individual bowls. Sprinkle the sunflower seeds on top.

Surprise Vegetable Almondine

The *surprising flavors of cooked cucumber and radish flank green beans and lightly browned leeks.*

Makes 4 servings

⅓ cup slivered almonds
1 tablespoon butter
¾ teaspoon salt
1 tablespoon vegetable oil
3 large leeks (white and tender green), well rinsed and thinly sliced
1 pound green beans, cut into thirds

1 bunch of radishes, diced
3 medium kirby cucumbers or 1 small cucumber, quartered lengthwise and sliced
2 teaspoons cornstarch
¾ cup vegetable broth
2 tablespoons dry vermouth or white wine
2 garlic cloves, minced

1) In a wok, cook the almonds over medium heat, stirring continuously, for 1 minute. Add ¼ teaspoon of the butter and a pinch of salt. Continue stirring, just until the almonds start to turn ivory, about 1 minute. Remove to a small bowl and set aside.

2) In the wok, melt the remaining butter with the oil. Add the leeks and green beans. Cook until the beans are half done, stirring frequently, about 3 minutes. Add the radishes and cucumbers and continue to cook until the cucumbers are warm but not mushy, about 2 minutes.

3) Mix the cornstarch and 2 tablespoons of the broth in a small bowl. Set aside. Add the remaining broth and salt, the vermouth, and the garlic to the vegetables. Bring to a boil, then stir the cornstarch mixture together and add it to the wok. Cook until the sauce just starts to thicken, about 1 minute. Add the almonds and stir to combine. Serve immediately.

Vietnamese Vegetable Stir-Fry

This light dish is unique as well as fun. Each diner wraps the vegetables and fresh mint in lettuce leaves and dips them in sauce. ***Makes 4 servings***

6 tablespoons soy sauce
2 tablespoons sugar
⅓ cup vegetable broth
2 garlic cloves, minced
1 tablespoon vegetable oil
2 leeks (white and tender green), well rinsed and chopped
1 teaspoon minced fresh ginger
1 carrot, thinly sliced
¼ pound fresh shiitake mushrooms, stemmed and thinly sliced
1 red bell pepper, thinly sliced

1 kirby or ½ small cucumber, halved lengthwise, seeds removed, thinly sliced
½ pound bean sprouts
¼ pound snow peas, sliced lengthwise
2 tablespoons lime juice
¼ teaspoon hot chili oil
1 large head of green leaf or romaine lettuce, separated into whole leaves
Lime wedges, for garnish
8 to 12 whole mint leaves

1) In a small bowl, combine 2 tablespoons of the soy sauce and 1 tablespoon of the sugar with the vegetable broth and garlic. Stir to mix well.

2) In a wok, heat the vegetable oil over high heat. Add the leeks and ginger and cook until the leeks start to soften, about 2 minutes. Add the carrot, shiitake mushrooms, bell pepper, and cucumber. Cook, stirring frequently, until the carrot is tender but still firm, about 5 minutes.

3) Reduce the heat to medium-low. Add the bean sprouts and snow peas, then immediately stir in the reserved sauce. Cover and cook just until the sprouts are slightly wilted, about 1 minute.

4) In a small attractive bowl, combine the remaining ¼ cup soy sauce and 1 tablespoon sugar with the lime juice and hot oil. Stir to dissolve the sugar. Serve the vegetables on one platter and the lettuce, dipping sauce, and lime wedges on another. To eat, place a small amount of the vegetable stir-fry in a large lettuce leaf; top with mint, then wrap. Dip in the sauce and eat.

Zucchini and Carrots with Tomato-Ginger Salsa

Ripe summer tomatoes turn *this into a spectacular dish.*

Makes 3 to 4 servings

2 large beefsteak tomatoes, finely chopped with their juices reserved
1 scallion, chopped
2½ tablespoons chopped cilantro
2 tablespoons soy sauce

2 teaspoons confectioners' sugar
1 teaspoon grated fresh ginger
3 tablespoons olive oil
3 medium zucchini, sliced
3 medium carrots, shredded
1 teaspoon salt

1) In a small bowl, combine the tomatoes and their juices with the scallion, cilantro, soy sauce, sugar, and ginger. Set the salsa aside.

2) In a wok, heat the oil over high heat for 1 minute. Add the zucchini and cook, stirring frequently and allowing some of the slices to brown, until the zucchini is tender but not mushy, 5 to 7 minutes. Add about three-fourths of the carrots and salt and cook, stirring, for 1 minute.

3) Serve on a platter or plate. Top with the tomato-ginger salsa and garnish with the remaining carrots.

From a Vegetarian Oven

*O*ven dishes have a
distinct advantage. For the most part, once prepared, they can be popped into the oven and left on
their own. That leaves the working cook at liberty
to set the table, sip some wine, or just collapse before
supper. Furthermore, most of these dishes can be
prepared ahead and baked at the last minute. Many
can even be cooked before serving and reheated,
or served at room temperature.

   The oven is a nice warm place for vegetables to
gather, marry, and make magic. The simplest vegetables are transformed into marvelous meatless
meals when the dry oven heat concentrates their
flavors. The recipes in this chapter use standard baking sheets or pans and several simple cooking

techniques: The vegetables are roasted; baked together in gratins, casseroles, and puddings; or paired with ready-made dough.

The delightful range of tastes and textures of oven-roasted vegetables may surprise the reader. Everyone knows how satisfying a baked potato can be. Now experience roasted garlic, mushrooms, tomatoes, beets, asparagus, and a myriad of other roasted vegetables. If you crave an antipasto-style dinner, try the Grand Vegetable Aioli or Italian Roasted Asparagus and Beets with Garlic-Bean Crostini. When roasting vegetables, be sure to lightly oil a baking sheet and to shake it or turn the vegetables occasionally to prevent sticking and facilitate cleanup.

Oven cooking deepens the flavors of gratin dishes, like Potato and Rutabaga Gratin or Yams and Greens Gratin with a Pecan Crust. Meals cooked in one baking dish, like Portobello Mushroom Lasagna and Summer Harvest Casserole, also make convenient company dishes because they are so easy to double or even triple. Just multiply the recipe and use a larger baking dish. If you are not sure your oven is accurate, purchase an oven thermometer at the supermarket or rely on the visual clues listed next to the cooking times.

And for the busy cook, readily available bread and pastry dough lends a hand. Purchasing pita, filo,

biscuit, and pizza dough saves a great deal of work, allowing you to create dishes that might otherwise be too time-consuming. Simple techniques for working with these doughs are included with each recipe. That makes it a snap to prepare great dishes like flaky Spinach and Feta Strudel, Mexican Pizza, Arugula and Roasted Pepper Stromboli, and Potato and Cheese Pizza.

Arugula and Roasted Pepper Stromboli

Purchase fresh or frozen dough
*in the supermarket to make this Italian favorite. Frozen dough
can be defrosted in the refrigerator overnight or left out at room
temperature until thawed.*   ***Makes 4 servings***

1½ tablespoons olive oil
2 tablespoons cornmeal
1 pound pizza or bread dough,
  thawed if frozen
¼ teaspoon crushed hot red
  pepper
1 bunch of arugula, tough stems
  removed, chopped

1 (4-ounce) jar roasted red
  peppers, chopped
1½ cups shredded Swiss cheese
¼ cup grated Romano cheese
1 egg

1) Preheat the oven to 450 degrees F. Lightly coat a large baking sheet
with the olive oil. Sprinkle the cornmeal evenly over the sheet.

2) On a flat work surface, stretch the pizza dough into a 12-inch square,
brush with olive oil, and sprinkle evenly with the hot pepper. Leaving a
½-inch border all around, sprinkle the arugula, roasted peppers, Swiss
cheese, and Romano cheese over the dough. Roll up.

3) In a small bowl, beat the egg with a fork. Brush over the Stromboli.
Set the Stromboli, seam-side down, on the baking sheet. Bake about
25 minutes, until the dough turns a dark golden brown and the bottom
sounds hollow when tapped.

Baked Parmesan Pancake with Fennel Confit

This unique, quickly assembled entrée, is a savory adaptation of a sweet German pancake. If the fennel comes with its dark green fronds attached, chop some to stir into the cooked confit and use some sprigs as garnish.   ***Makes 4 servings***

2 small fennel bulbs, sliced
2 teaspoons olive oil
2 garlic cloves, sliced
¼ teaspoon salt
Crushed hot red pepper
3 tablespoons butter

3 tablespoons grated Parmesan
  cheese
½ cup flour
½ cup milk
2 eggs
4 lemon wedges

1) Preheat the oven to 425 degrees F. Remove the outer stalks from the fennel bulbs and discard. Trim the fennel. Cut the bulbs in half lengthwise and thinly slice. Place a large piece of foil on the counter. Spread the fennel over the foil and sprinkle the olive oil, garlic, salt, a pinch of hot pepper, and 1 tablespoon water on top. Mix with your hands and loosely enclose the fennel in a foil package. Place in the oven for 15 minutes.

2) In a large ovenproof skillet, preferably cast-iron, melt the butter over medium heat. Reduce the heat to low and keep warm while you prepare the batter. If the butter lightly browns, it will add a nutty taste to the pancake.

3) In a medium bowl, combine 1 tablespoon of the Parmesan cheese with the flour, milk, eggs, and a pinch of salt and hot pepper. With a wooden spoon, lightly mix; there will still be lumps. With a rubber spatula, scrape the mixture into the warm pan and immediately place in the oven, next to the fennel confit.

4) Bake until the pancake is browned and lightly puffed, about 20 minutes. Immediately sprinkle with the remaining 2 tablespoons Parmesan cheese. Cut the pancake into 4 wedges and serve with the fennel confit and lemon wedges.

Bulgur Stuffed Mushrooms

Dried shiitakes can usually be found in the Asian section of supermarkets, in health food stores, and in specialty food shops. They add a meaty wild taste to mellow cultivated mushrooms. This dish can be prepared the day ahead, refrigerated, and baked at the last minute.

Makes 3 to 4 servings

½ cup bulgur
6 dried medium shiitake
  mushrooms
12 large stuffing mushrooms
  (1½ pounds)
2½ tablespoons olive oil
¼ cup chopped shallots
½ teaspoon dried thyme leaves

1 tablespoon chopped parsley
  (optional)
½ teaspoon salt
¼ teaspoon freshly ground
  pepper
¼ cup grated Parmesan cheese
4 lemon wedges

1) Preheat the oven to 425 degrees F. Place the bulgur in a medium bowl. Cover with boiling water and soak for 30 minutes. Drain through a fine sieve, pressing out any extra water. Return the bulgur to the bowl.

2) Meanwhile, in a small heatproof bowl, cover the dried shiitake mushrooms with 1 cup boiling water and let stand until softened, about 15 minutes. Cut off and discard the stems. Chop the caps.

3) Wipe the stuffing mushrooms clean with a damp paper towel. Remove the stems. Set the caps aside and finely chop the stems.

4) In a 12-inch ovenproof skillet, heat 1½ tablespoons oil over medium heat. Add the shallots, chopped stuffing mushroom stems, shiitake mushrooms, and thyme. Cook, stirring occasionally, until the mushrooms are tender, about 5 minutes. Add the mushroom mixture to the bulgur, along with the remaining 1 tablespoon olive oil, parsley, salt, and pepper. Stuff the mushrooms very full with about 2 tablespoons filling each.

5) Rinse out the skillet, leaving about 2 tablespoons of water in the pan. Arrange the mushrooms in a single layer, packed closely together. Bring to a simmer over medium heat, cover tightly with a lid or with foil, and bake until the mushrooms are tender all the way through, about 15 minutes.

6) Remove the mushrooms from the oven and turn the heat up to broil. Sprinkle the cheese over the tops of the mushrooms, place the skillet about 4 inches from the heat, and broil until the cheese browns a little, 2 to 3 minutes. Serve with lemon wedges.

Savory Corn Pudding with Tomato Salsa

While the cheese browns on top, the soft cornmeal stays at the bottom of the pudding here, creating a pleasing contrast of taste and texture. An 8-inch baking dish will yield a creamy pudding, while a larger gratin will produce a firmer pudding with a crisper top. Either way, this is sure to be a favorite. If you are in a bind for time, accompany with store-bought salsa. Low-fat or whole milk and cheese work equally well in this pudding. ***Makes 4 servings***

2 large tomatoes, chopped
⅓ cup minced shallots
2 tablespoons chopped cilantro
  or parsley
2 garlic cloves, minced
1 to 2 jalapeño peppers, to taste,
  seeded and minced, or
  ⅛ teaspoon cayenne
1¼ teaspoons salt
½ cup yellow cornmeal
1 tablespoon sugar
1½ teaspoons baking powder

1 teaspoon dry mustard
¼ teaspoon cayenne
Pinch of dried oregano
2 tablespoons butter, cut into
  thin slices
2 cups milk
1½ cups fresh or frozen corn
  kernels
3 eggs
½ cup shredded Cheddar or
  Monterey jack cheese

1) Preheat the oven to 350 degrees F. In a small bowl, mix the tomatoes with 1½ tablespoons shallots, 1 tablespoon cilantro, half the garlic, the jalapeños, and a pinch of the salt. Set the fresh salsa aside at room temperature.

2) In a large bowl, combine the cornmeal, remaining shallots and garlic, sugar, baking powder, remaining salt, mustard, cayenne, and oregano.

3) In a large glass measure or other microwave-safe bowl, microwave the butter on High until mostly melted, about 1 minute. Add the milk and heat until the milk is hot and the butter completely melted, about 2 minutes. Gradually pour into the cornmeal mixture, whisking to remove lumps. Stir in the corn, eggs, and remaining 1 tablespoon cilantro.

4) Pour the pudding base into a lightly buttered 8-inch-square baking dish or oval gratin. Bake 30 minutes. Sprinkle the Cheddar cheese evenly over the pudding. Increase the oven temperature to 375 degrees F and bake about 15 minutes longer, until the pudding is set and the cheese is lightly browned on top. Serve hot with the salsa.

Grand Vegetable Aioli

This is a vegetarian adaptation of a Provençale party dish, lovingly described by Mireille Johnston in her book The Cuisine of the Sun. *It utilizes simple raw and cooked vegetables as a foil for a potent garlic mayonnaise spiked with fresh lemon. Those with a spicy palette might enjoy adding a couple of teaspoons of curry powder to the aioli.*

For those who have never attempted a homemade mayonnaise, the food processor method I suggest makes it foolproof. This dish is easy to halve, double, or triple. It's a great do-ahead summer party dish—stunning set out on a large platter or wooden cutting board. ***Makes 8 servings***

4 large red or gold waxy
   potatoes, halved and thickly
   sliced lengthwise
¾ cup plus 2 tablespoons olive oil
2 pounds asparagus, tough ends
   removed
¾ teaspoon salt
2 eggs
5 garlic cloves, crushed
1 tablespoon grainy mustard

¾ cup vegetable oil
1½ tablespoons fresh lemon
   juice
Dash of cayenne
3 carrots, cut into sticks
3 celery ribs, cut into sticks
3 ripe plum tomatoes, cut into
   wedges
1 yellow bell pepper, cut into
   thick strips

1) Preheat the oven to 425 degrees F. In a large bowl, toss the potatoes with 1 tablespoon olive oil to coat. Place on a large baking sheet in a single layer. Roast for 5 minutes. Toss the asparagus in 1 tablespoon olive oil and add to the baking sheet in a single layer. (If your baking sheet is too small, use a second one.) Continue to roast until the potatoes are brown and crisp and the asparagus is tender but still firm, about 12 minutes longer. Season the potatoes and asparagus with ½ teaspoon of the salt.

2) While the vegetables are roasting, make the aioli: Add the eggs, garlic, mustard, and remaining ¼ teaspoon salt to a food processor. Blend until well combined and a little frothy, about 30 seconds. With the machine on, slowly pour in the remaining ¾ cup olive oil and then the vegetable oil in a thin stream. Finish by adding the lemon juice. Season with the cayenne and additional salt to taste. Transfer to a small serving bowl or sauceboat.

3) To serve, place the bowl filled with the aioli on a large platter. Surround with the potatoes, asparagus, carrots, celery, tomatoes, and bell pepper, arranging them decoratively. Serve warm or at room temperature. Using tongs, diners help themselves to a little of each vegetable along with a large spoonful of aioli.

Italian Roasted Asparagus and Beets with Garlic-Bean Crostini

This colorful antipasto platter makes a complete meal—earthy asparagus and sweet beets served with garlicky beans spread on toasted Italian bread. Roasting these vegetables deepens their flavors. Coarse kosher salt is particularly good with roasted vegetables; if you don't have any, use half as much regular salt.   ***Makes 4 servings***

1 (19-ounce) can cannellini or other large white beans, rinsed and drained
3 tablespoons plus 2 teaspoons olive oil
2 tablespoons grated Romano cheese
2 garlic cloves, crushed
½ teaspoon coarse (kosher) salt
⅛ teaspoon freshly ground pepper
1 loaf of Italian or French bread, sliced
1 large bunch of beets
1 pound medium asparagus, tough ends removed
4 lemon wedges

1) Preheat the oven to 400 degrees F. In a food processor, combine the beans, 2 tablespoons of the olive oil, the cheese, garlic, and a pinch of salt and pepper. Puree until completely smooth. Using a rubber spatula, scrape into a small bowl or serving crock.

2) Place the sliced bread on a large baking sheet; brush the tops lightly with 1 tablespoon of the olive oil. Bake 5 to 7 minutes, until lightly toasted. Remove to a basket and set aside. Leave the oven on. Shake any crumbs off the baking sheet.

3) Remove the beet tops and roots. Peel the beets, then cut in half and slice ¼ to ½ inch thick. In a medium bowl, toss the beet slices with 1 teaspoon of the olive oil. Spread in a single layer across half of the baking sheet. Roast for 10 minutes.

4) Meanwhile, cut the tough stem ends off the asparagus and toss the spears with the remaining 1 teaspoon olive oil. After 10 minutes, shake the baking sheet to loosen the beet slices. Add the asparagus in a single layer to the other half of the baking sheet. Roast until both the beets and asparagus are tender, 10 to 15 minutes.

5) Set the bowl of garlic-bean puree in the center of a serving platter. Arrange the beets and asparagus around the puree. Season the vegetables with the remaining salt and pepper. Garnish with the lemon wedges and pass the toasts on the side.

Summer Harvest Casserole

This dish, from my friend Jane McWhorter, is particularly pretty prepared in a glass loaf pan, so you can see all the colorful layers of vegetables.

Makes 4 to 5 servings

2 teaspoons olive oil
2 small zucchini, sliced
1 small yellow squash, sliced
½ teaspoon salt
½ teaspoon freshly ground
　pepper
1 medium onion, sliced

3 large tomatoes, sliced
¼ cup chopped fresh basil
¼ cup chopped parsley
⅔ cup Italian-seasoned bread
　crumbs
2 cups shredded Monterey jack
　cheese

1) Preheat the oven to 400 degrees F. Rub a 9-by-5-by-3-inch loaf pan, preferably glass, with the oil.

2) Layer half the zucchini and yellow squash in the loaf pan. Season with half the salt and pepper. Layer on half the onion, tomatoes, basil, parsley, bread crumbs, and cheese. Press down firmly on the vegetables. Repeat the layering with the remaining ingredients. The vegetables may come over the top, so press down firmly and cover tightly with foil.

3) Set on a sheet pan and bake for 40 minutes. Uncover and continue to bake for 10 minutes, or until the cheese is lightly browned on top.

Portobello Mushroom Lasagna

Because the pasta doesn't have to be cooked first, this lasagna is a breeze to assemble.

Makes 6 servings

1¼ cups ricotta cheese
1 egg
¾ teaspoon salt
1 (8-ounce) package sliced portobello mushroom caps or 10 ounces portobello mushrooms, stems discarded, caps sliced ½ inch thick
1 small onion, chopped
3 tablespoons olive oil
2 garlic cloves, minced

1 teaspoon freshly ground pepper
5 large plum tomatoes, quartered
1 (14½-ounce) can Italian-style stewed tomatoes
2½ teaspoons dried oregano
9 lasagna noodles
8 ounces mozzarella cheese, thinly sliced, or 1 (8-ounce) package shredded mozzarella cheese
⅔ cup grated Parmesan cheese

1) Preheat the oven to 375 degrees F. In a small bowl, blend the ricotta, egg, and ¼ teaspoon salt. Set the ricotta filling aside.

2) In an 11-by-7-inch baking dish, toss the portobello mushrooms, onion, 2 tablespoons olive oil, and garlic with the pepper and remaining ½ teaspoon salt. Roast for 10 minutes. Stir, add the plum tomatoes, and roast 5 minutes longer. Add the roasted mushrooms and tomatoes to a large bowl along with the stewed tomatoes, ⅔ cup water, and the oregano.

3) Rinse out the baking dish, wipe dry, and coat with the remaining 1 tablespoon oil. Evenly layer in this order: half the mushroom-tomato sauce, 3 dry lasagna noodles, all the ricotta filling, half the mozzarella cheese, half the Parmesan cheese, 3 more noodles, the remaining sauce, and the remaining 3 noodles, pressing them into the sauce. Lastly, top with the remainder of the mozzarella and Parmesan cheeses.

4) Cover tightly and bake for 35 minutes. Uncover and bake until the liquid is absorbed, about 15 minutes. Let stand 10 minutes before serving.

Chèvre Pizza with Pesto

Chèvre *is simply the French word for goat cheese and any soft fresh goat cheese will work here, whether French or one of our excellent American brands. Although any pita will do as a base here, for a great crust, use the slightly thicker "pocketless" pitas, which are buckled rather than flat. This kind of pita can be found in the deli department of most supermarkets.*

For appetizers or snacks, cut the pitas into wedges. This goat cheese pizza freezes well either before or after it is baked, making it handy for drop-in guests. Low- or reduced-fat substitutions can be used for the chèvre and sour cream.

Makes 6 servings

1½ cups basil pesto
6 white or whole wheat
   "pocketless" pitas
¾ cup fresh goat cheese
½ cup sour cream

1¼ cups grated Parmesan
   cheese, preferably freshly
   grated
2 tablespoons chopped fresh
   basil or parsley

1) Set racks in the top and bottom thirds of the oven. Preheat the oven to 450 degrees F.

2) If the pesto is oily, drain off any extra oil. Spread the pesto evenly over each pita, leaving a 1-inch border all around the edges. In a small bowl, blend the goat cheese with the sour cream. Using 2 spoons, drop the mixture in dollops evenly over the pesto. Sprinkle the Parmesan cheese over the pizzas, pressing down gently with the back of a spoon to flatten the goat cheese.

3) Bake the pizzas directly on the top rack of the oven, with a baking sheet on the rack below to catch any drips, until hot and crisp, about 10 minutes. Sprinkle 1 teaspoon chopped basil over each pita and serve immediately.

Mexican Pizza

This is a reduced-fat pizza with plenty of pizzazz. One tablespoon of minced pickled jalapeños that have been rinsed of their brine can be used to replace the fresh jalapeños. **_Makes 4 servings_**

4 medium plum tomatoes, finely
   chopped
1 small onion, chopped
¼ cup chopped cilantro
¼ teaspoon salt
2 to 3 jalapeño peppers, seeded
   and minced

4 "pocketless" pitas
1 cup shredded Monterey jack or
   Cheddar cheese
½ cup grated Parmesan cheese

1) Set racks in the top and bottom thirds of the oven. Preheat the oven to 450 degrees F.

2) In a small bowl, mix the tomatoes, onion, cilantro, salt, and jalapeño peppers to taste. Spread the tomato mixture over the pitas, leaving a 1-inch border all around the bread. Sprinkle ¼ cup Monterey jack and 2 tablespoons Parmesan cheese on top of each.

3) Bake the pizzas directly on the top rack of the oven, with a baking sheet on the rack below to catch any drips, until hot and crisp, about 10 minutes. Serve immediately.

Potato and Cheese Pizza

This white pizza is a
carbohydrate lover's dream come true: potatoes and bread,
seasoned with Italian herbs and a touch of cheese. My students
adore it. Defrost the pizza dough by leaving it at room
temperature for a few hours, or in the refrigerator overnight. Serve
with a tossed salad or marinated vegetables. **Makes 4 servings**

3 tablespoons cornmeal
1 pound frozen pizza dough,
  thawed
1 pound red potatoes, scrubbed
  and very thinly sliced
1 tablespoon olive oil
1 teaspoon dried rosemary
¼ teaspoon dried sage

¼ teaspoon dried oregano
½ teaspoon coarse salt
½ teaspoon freshly ground
  pepper
1 cup shredded mild cheese,
  such as Gouda or Swiss
½ medium red onion, thinly
  sliced

1) Preheat the oven to 475 degrees F. Set the rack in the upper third of
the oven. Coat a large baking sheet liberally with nonstick cooking spray
or oil. Sprinkle cornmeal evenly over the sheet. Place the dough on the sheet.
Using your hands, press the dough out evenly to cover as much of the
sheet as possible.

2) In a medium bowl, toss together the potatoes, oil, rosemary, sage,
oregano, salt, and pepper. Spoon the potato mixture onto the dough,
using your hands to spread or neatly "shingle" the potatoes, overlapping
them as little as possible, and leaving a 1-inch border of dough all
around. Sprinkle with the cheese and onion. Bake until the potatoes are
cooked through and lightly browned and the crust is crisp, about
20 minutes.

Dinner Baked Potatoes Stuffed with Cottage Cheese and Scallions

Love baked potatoes with *sour cream and chives? This low-fat version is one of my students' favorites. If pressed for time, this recipe can be made in the microwave. The taste is good, but the potatoes won't get crisp. For a compromise, cook the potatoes in the microwave, but reheat the stuffed potatoes in the oven, for a total cooking time of about 25 minutes.* **Makes 4 servings**

5 large baking potatoes (about ¾ pound each)
1 cup cottage cheese
½ (10-ounce) package frozen chopped spinach, thawed and squeezed dry

2 scallions, finely chopped
¾ teaspoon salt
½ teaspoon freshly ground pepper
3 tablespoons grated Parmesan or shredded Cheddar cheese

1) Preheat the oven to 400 degrees F. Scrub, dry, and prick each potato several times with a fork. Place in the oven and bake until soft all the way through, 50 to 60 minutes.

2) Using kitchen mitts to handle the hot potatoes, cut a small slice lengthwise off the top of each potato. Using a spoon, scrape the potato off the top pieces and discard the skin; then scoop out each potato, leaving a little on the sides to help them hold their shape. Set aside the inside of the potatoes in a medium bowl. Place the 4 largest potato skins on a small baking sheet; discard the other one or save for another use.

3) Mash the potatoes well. Stir in the cottage cheese, spinach, scallions, salt, and pepper. Season with additional salt and pepper to taste.

4) Using your hands, scoop up 4 equal-size oval mounds of the potato mixture. Stuff each one into a potato skin; they should be heaping. Press to secure. Sprinkle the cheese on top. Set the baking sheet in the oven and bake about 25 to 30 minutes, until the potatoes are hot all the way through and the cheese on top is melted and starting to brown.

Potato and Rutabaga Gratin

This is a variation on scalloped
potatoes, the classic holiday accompaniment to a large roast.
But times have changed. This rich and satisfying dish need not
accompany meat. In fact, this gratin, paired with a simple
green salad, is one of my family's favorite winter meals. If you use
a food processor to slice the vegetables, this dish is a snap.

Makes 6 servings

2 tablespoons butter
5 medium baking potatoes
  (about 2½ pounds), peeled
  and sliced
½ small rutabaga (about ¾
  pound), peeled and sliced
1 small red onion, thinly sliced

3 garlic cloves, thinly sliced
1½ teaspoons salt
¼ teaspoon freshly ground
  pepper
2 cups shredded Swiss cheese
1½ cups hot milk

1) Preheat the oven to 425 degrees F. Set the rack in the upper third of
the oven. Grease a 13-by-9-inch baking dish with 1 tablespoon of the
butter and set aside.

2) In a large bowl, toss the potatoes with the rutabaga, red onion, garlic,
salt, pepper, and half the cheese. Turn into the baking dish. Pour the hot
milk over the potatoes and press down so that as much of the potatoes as
possible are covered by milk. Top with the remaining cheese and dot
with the remaining butter.

3) Bake 40 to 45 minutes, until the gratin is bubbly and browned on top.

Texts Tortilla Pie

Here is instant Tex-Mex food. *The ingredients are tossed in a bowl, layered like lasagna, and baked for 15 minutes. This is a great back-up "pantry meal," since all the ingredients can be kept in the cupboard.* **Makes 4 servings**

½ cup instant brown rice
⅔ cup boiling water
1 (14½-ounce) can kidney beans, rinsed and drained
1 (8-ounce) can tomato sauce
1 (4-ounce) can chopped green chiles, drained
1 small onion, chopped
1 tablespoon chili powder
1 teaspoon ground cumin

¼ teaspoon cayenne
1 (2¼-ounce) can sliced ripe olives, drained
4 corn tortillas
1 teaspoon vegetable oil
1¾ cups shredded Mexican cheese blend or Cheddar cheese
1 small avocado, sliced
Sour cream

1) Place the brown rice in a small heatproof bowl and cover with the boiling water. Cover the bowl and let stand for 10 minutes, or until all the water is absorbed.

2) Preheat the oven to 400 degrees F. In a large bowl, combine the kidney beans, tomato sauce, green chiles, onion, chili powder, cumin, and cayenne. Reserve 1 tablespoon of the olives; add the remainder of the can to the bowl and toss to mix the bean sauce well.

3) Lay 1 tortilla in the bottom of a lightly oiled 8-inch round cake pan. Cover with one-fourth of the bean sauce and one-fourth of the cheese. Add another tortilla, one-fourth of the bean sauce, ½ cup rice, and one-fourth of the cheese. Add the third tortilla, one-fourth of the bean sauce, the remaining rice, and one-fourth of the cheese. Add the last tortilla and cover with the remaining bean sauce. Decorate the top of the pie with the sliced avocado. Top with the reserved olives and remaining cheese.

4) Bake for 15 minutes, or until the cheese is melted and the pie is piping hot. Pass a bowl of sour cream on the side.

Spinach and Feta Strudel

This version of a Greek spinach pie takes the mystery out of filo dough. It is a great party dish either as a main course or cut into small pieces as an appetizer. Filo dough can be found in the freezer section at the supermarket. To defrost the filo and spinach, leave them in the refrigerator overnight, or at room temperature for several hours. The spinach can also be thawed in a covered glass bowl in a microwave on High for 2 to 4 minutes. **Makes 4 to 6 servings**

1 (10-ounce) package frozen chopped spinach, thawed
1¼ cups crumbled feta cheese (about 4½ ounces)
2 scallions, chopped
¼ cup plus 2 tablespoons chopped fresh dill
¼ cup chopped parsley
½ teaspoon salt
¼ teaspoon freshly ground pepper

2 eggs
1 tablespoon butter
3 tablespoons olive oil
1 tablespoon Dijon mustard
8 sheets of filo dough, thawed if frozen
1 cup plain yogurt
Dill sprigs, for garnish

1) Preheat the oven to 350 degrees F. Drain excess water from the spinach and place in a large kitchen towel. Squeeze out all extra water; there will be a lot.

2) In a medium bowl, thoroughly blend the spinach, feta, scallions, ¼ cup chopped dill, parsley, ¼ teaspoon salt, and the pepper. Add the eggs and mix again.

3) Combine the butter and oil in a small microwaveproof bowl and heat until the butter is just melted, about 1 minute on High. Add the mustard and stir with a pastry brush. Set aside the bowl with the brush in it.

4) Place a slightly damp kitchen towel on the counter and unroll the filo dough onto the towel. Cover the top of the filo with another damp towel, replacing the top towel continuously as you work to prevent the dough from drying out. Remove the first sheet of dough and place on the counter with a short side on the bottom. Brush very lightly with the mustard mixture. Repeat with 6 more layers. (Don't worry if the filo occasionally breaks or crumbles; just patch it as best you can.) Place the last sheet of filo on top, but don't brush with the mustard mixture.

5) Place the spinach mixture in a line along the bottom of the dough, leaving a 1-inch border along the bottom and sides. Carefully roll the dough up tightly, tucking the ends in as you roll. When you are finished, place the log-shaped strudel on a lightly oiled baking sheet and brush with the remaining mustard mixture. Bake 40 minutes, or until well browned and crisp. Let rest 5 minutes.

6) In a small bowl, combine the yogurt with the remaining 2 tablespoons chopped dill and ¼ teaspoon salt. To serve, cut the strudel with a serrated knife into 1-inch-thick slices. Serve each person several slices with some sauce. Garnish with a sprig of dill.

Roasted Rosemary Vegetables

Roasting caramelizes the natural sugars in vegetables and eliminates some of the excess moisture, both intensifying and heightening their flavor.

Makes 4 servings

1 red bell pepper, cut into
  8 pieces
1 yellow bell pepper, cut into
  8 pieces
4 carrots, cut into ½-inch slices
¾ teaspoon freshly ground
  pepper
½ teaspoon dried rosemary

2 garlic cloves, minced
1 Spanish onion, cut into ½-inch
  slices
1½ pounds new potatoes, cut
  into 1-inch wedges
1 tablespoon olive oil
½ teaspoon coarse (kosher) salt

1) Preheat the oven to 425 degrees F. Toss everything together except the salt. Spread out the vegetables in a single layer on the largest baking sheet you have.

2) Roast for 10 minutes; then shake the baking sheet so the vegetables don't stick. Continue to roast until the potatoes are tender and lightly browned, about 15 minutes longer. Toss with the salt and serve.

Vegetable Cobbler

In this savory version of a fruit cobbler, creamy vegetables are topped with store-bought biscuit dough. Mini-carrots can be purchased in a bag in the produce section of the supermarket. **Makes 4 servings**

3 medium red potatoes (about ¾ pound), cut into small dice
1 cup mini-carrots
2 celery ribs, sliced
1 tablespoon butter
2 tablespoons oil
1 large onion, chopped
1 (8-ounce) package sliced mushrooms or ½ pound medium mushrooms, sliced
1¼ teaspoons dried tarragon leaves
¼ teaspoon salt
⅛ teaspoon freshly ground pepper
⅓ cup flour
2½ cups nonfat milk
1 cup fresh or frozen peas
1 (12-ounce) package biscuit dough

1) Preheat the oven to 400 degrees F. In a large ovenproof skillet, combine 2 quarts water with the potatoes, carrots, and celery. Bring to a boil and cover. Reduce the heat to medium and cook until the potatoes are almost cooked through, about 5 minutes. Drain, reserving the vegetables in the colander.

2) In same skillet, melt the butter and oil. Add the onion, mushrooms, tarragon, salt, and pepper. Cook, stirring frequently, until the mushrooms are wilted and the onions are soft, about 5 minutes. Sprinkle the flour over the mushrooms. Reduce the heat to low and cook, stirring continuously for 2 minutes, to cook the flour. Slowly add the milk, stirring well until the sauce is thickened, about 5 minutes. Add the peas and return the partially cooked vegetables to the skillet. Cook over medium heat until thickened, about 2 minutes. Season with additional salt and pepper to taste, if desired.

3) Evenly space pieces of the biscuit dough on top of the vegetables. Bake until the biscuits are fluffy and browned on top, about 20 minutes.

Whole Wheat Bread Pudding with Broccoli and Cheddar

This homey, savory bread pudding makes a great brunch dish. A crisp green salad is a fine accompaniment. *Makes 4 to 6 servings*

5 slices of whole wheat bread, toasted until crisp
1 tablespoon vegetable oil
1 small head of broccoli, cut into ½-inch florets
3 eggs
2¼ cups milk

1 small onion, grated
¼ teaspoon salt
¼ teaspoon freshly ground pepper
1½ cups shredded Cheddar or Swiss cheese

1) Preheat the oven to 350 degrees F. Overlap the bread slices in the bottom of an oiled 13-by-9-inch baking dish. Sprinkle the broccoli evenly over the bread.

2) In a medium bowl, whisk together the eggs, milk, onion, salt, pepper, and half the cheese and pour on top of the bread. Sprinkle with the remaining cheese. Bake until the pudding is set, about 30 minutes. Let stand for 5 minutes before serving.

Yams and Greens Gratin with a Pecan Crust

Before cooking the greens, *remove the tough ends and center spines. Chop them either by hand or by pulsing in a food processor.* **Makes 4 to 6 servings**

2½ pounds yams (about 4), peeled and thinly sliced
1 teaspoon salt
½ teaspoon freshly ground pepper
½ teaspoon dried sage
½ teaspoon dried thyme
2 tablespoons butter
2½ tablespoons olive oil
1 Spanish onion, sliced

3 garlic cloves, minced
1 small bunch of collard greens, coarsely chopped
1 small bunch of mustard greens, coarsely chopped
1 (14½-ounce) can vegetable broth
2 slices of whole wheat bread
1 cup pecans

1) Preheat the oven to 425 degrees F. In a large bowl, toss the yams with ½ teaspoon salt, the pepper, sage, and thyme.

2) In a 13-by-9-inch flameproof gratin dish or the equivalent, melt the butter with 2 tablespoons oil over medium heat. Add the onion and garlic and cook, stirring, until the onion is translucent, about 5 minutes. Add the greens gradually, turning with tongs, until they are all added and wilted, about 5 minutes. Stir in the remaining ½ teaspoon salt.

3) In a large bowl, toss the wilted greens with the yams. Place back in the gratin dish. Pour in the vegetable broth and bring to a boil over high heat. Press the yams down into the liquid, cover well with foil, and bake until the yams are tender, about 30 minutes.

4) In a food processor, combine the bread, pecans, and the remaining 1½ teaspoons oil. Pulse a few times until the pecans are very coarsely chopped. Cover the yams with the pecan topping and cook until crisp, about 15 minutes. Let stand for 10 to 15 minutes before serving.

Salad of Field Greens with Roasted Garlic and Goat Cheese Croutons

Mixed salad greens are sometimes called field greens or mesclun. Now widely available in many quality supermarkets, they are a mixture of small washed lettuces, balanced for flavor and texture. For an easy substitute, make your own mix. Just combine mild lettuces, like Boston and green leaf, with tangy arugula, radicchio, or Belgian endive.

Whole garlic bulbs mellow considerably during roasting, so don't be put off by the whole head served to each person. Each diner assembles their own garlic croutons by squeezing the garlic out of the cloves onto toasted bread. ***Makes 4 servings***

4 heads of garlic, preferably
   without green sprouts
¼ cup olive oil
⅛ teaspoon thyme leaves
⅛ teaspoon salt
⅛ teaspoon freshly ground pepper

1 tablespoon red wine vinegar
1 teaspoon mustard
1 baguette, thinly sliced
4 ounces soft white goat cheese,
   preferably a log
¾ pound field greens

1) Preheat the oven to 400 degrees F. Slice enough off the top of each head to expose the garlic "flesh," about ½ inch. Toss the heads in 1½ teaspoons of olive oil, the thyme, and a pinch of salt and pepper. Wrap the heads loosely in foil and roast until you can easily squeeze the puree out of 1 clove, about 40 minutes.

2) In a small bowl, combine the vinegar and mustard. With a fork or whisk, add the remaining salt, pepper, and 3½ tablespoons olive oil. Set aside.

3) Toast the bread on a baking sheet until warm and starting to crisp, about 3 to 5 minutes. Spread the goat cheese over half of these croutons.

4) In a large bowl, toss the dressing with the field greens. To serve, place some of the dressed greens, goat cheese croutons, remaining toasted bread, and a head of roasted garlic on each of 4 plates. The garlic is squeezed out of its skin and spread over the toasted bread.

Warm Avocado and Goat Cheese Salad with Spicy Lime-Tomato Dressing

Mexican or Californian *avocados, with bumpy skins, are perfect for this luxurious luncheon salad. Green leaf lettuce has a very curly leaf.*

Makes 4 servings

4 plum tomatoes, chopped
2 tablespoons fresh lime juice
2 garlic cloves, minced
2 tablespoons chopped cilantro
½ teaspoon crushed hot red pepper
1 tablespoon vegetable oil

2 ripe avocados
Salt
¼ cup soft white goat cheese
1 small baguette, thinly sliced
8 leaves of green leaf lettuce
4 lime wedges

1) Preheat the oven to 350 degrees F. In a medium bowl, stir together the tomatoes, lime juice, garlic, cilantro, hot peppers, and oil. Set the dressing aside.

2) With a paring knife, carefully halve both avocados lengthwise around their pits. Pull them apart, remove the pits, and using a tablespoon, carefully separate the flesh from the skin, but leave the avocado in the skin.

3) Place the 4 avocado halves on a lightly oiled baking sheet. Season lightly with salt. Fill each center with 1 tablespoon of the goat cheese. Spread the bread slices over the rest of the baking sheet.

4) Bake about 10 minutes, until the avocado is warmed through and the bread is lightly toasted.

5) Arrange 2 lettuce leaves on each plate. Set the warm avocado on top. Spoon some of the dressing around each avocado and a little on top. Distribute the warm toasts on each plate and garnish with a lime wedge. Serve immediately.

From the Vegetarian Saucepan and Steamer

A saucepan is a heavy, deep, straight-sided pot—the workhorse of the kitchen. It is used both covered and uncovered to cook a wide variety of foods. Medium or large saucepans are most useful for the recipes in this chapter. They not only accommodate the food easily, but also allow extra space for stirring, boiling without spillage, and for the insertion of a steamer basket.

The addition of a steamer basket transforms a saucepan into a different pot altogether. Steaming allows vegetables to retain their flavor, color, and nutrients. Better yet, a complete vegetarian dinner can be steamed in as little as five minutes.

Steaming is a simple procedure that needs no fancy

155

equipment. There are many varieties of steamers, from those specially designed for specific saucepans to inexpensive flexiblé steamers, which can be purchased at most supermarkets, hardware, and kitchen supply stores. I find a flexible steamer, with its perforated leaves, extremely useful. Because it can open and close to change size, it fits any kind of pot and will accommodate both small and large meals. If no steamer is available, a make-shift steamer can be assembled by inserting a small metal colander into a large pot.

The principles of steaming are basic. Water is added to the bottom of a saucepan with a steamer in place. Add enough so that it doesn't boil away during cooking, but not enough to touch the vegetables, or they will boil instead of steam. Usually one to two inches is sufficient. Simply bring the water to a boil, add the vegetables to the steamer, and tightly cover the pan. Steam until the vegetables are tender but still firm and brightly colored. Bear in mind that foods will continue to cook a little after they are removed from the pot, so it is better to undercook slightly rather than overcook.

A platter of steamed vegetables with a sauce or dip makes a healthy and satisfying meal, There are an exciting variety of international steamed vegetable dishes in this chapter, including Hummus with

ONE-POT VEGETARIAN DISHES

Steamed Vegetables, Vegetable Fondue with a cheesy dip, and Red Russian Vegetables with Dill and Caraway.

Without the steamer, the saucepan is an ideal place to cook grains, a staple in the vegetarian diet. Familiar grains like rice, as well as less common grains, like bulgur and wheat berries, become quick one-pot meals when they are combined with a wide variety of vegetables. Conveniently, most of these grains are now available in the supermarket, although a few must be purchased in the health food store.

Be sure to sample the grain-based dishes in this chapter, like Sweet Pepper Pilaf with Broccoli and Black Beans or Collards and Rice. Or savor other great saucepan meals, like low-fat Steamed Eggplant with Sweet Pepper Relish, Spaghetti Squash with Marinara Sauce, or the sweet summer taste of Fresh Corn Salad with Cilantro Vinaigrette.

Asparagus and Couscous with Orange-Sesame Vinaigrette

The time to make a meal out of asparagus is in the spring, when they are at their peak. This technique for making couscous is always a hit with my students.

Makes 4 servings

2 pounds fresh asparagus
¼ cup orange juice, preferably fresh
1 tablespoon rice vinegar or red wine vinegar
1 teaspoon orange zest
1 teaspoon soy sauce

1 tablespoon vegetable oil
2 teaspoons Asian sesame oil
¼ teaspoon salt
1 teaspoon butter or oil
1 cup couscous
2 teaspoons sesame seeds
1 orange, halved and sliced

1) To prepare the asparagus, snap 1 stalk; this will remove the tough part. Line up the rest of the asparagus and cut them the same length as the first stalk. In a large saucepan, bring 1½ inches water to a boil. Place the asparagus in a steamer over the water and cook until tender but still firm, 7 to 10 minutes.

2) Meanwhile, in a small bowl, combine the orange juice, vinegar, orange zest, and soy sauce. Whisk in the vegetable oil and sesame oil until well blended. Set the orange-sesame vinaigrette aside.

3) When the asparagus are done, transfer them to a colander and cover with a kitchen towel to keep warm. Rinse the pot briefly, then add 1⅓ cups water and bring to a boil over high heat. Add the salt and butter. As soon as the butter melts, stir in the couscous, cover, and remove from the heat. Let stand 5 minutes.

4) Fluff up the couscous and turn it out onto a serving platter. Top with the asparagus spears and sprinkle the sesame seeds over the asparagus. Garnish with the orange slices. Pass the vinaigrette on the side as a dipping sauce.

Barley Risotto with Wild Mushrooms and Sun-Dried Tomatoes

Risotto is typically a rich northern Italian rice dish that has to be stirred for 20 minutes or so. This unorthodox but tasty version is made with barley and is much simpler to make. Barley can be found next to the dried beans in the supermarket.

Makes 4 to 5 servings

5 sun-dried tomato halves
1 tablespoon olive oil
2 leeks (white and tender green), well rinsed and chopped
4 garlic cloves, minced
⅓ pound fresh shiitake mushrooms, stemmed, caps sliced

1 cup pearl barley
2¼ cups canned vegetable broth
¼ cup dry vermouth or white wine
1 tablespoon butter
⅓ cup grated Parmesan cheese
¼ teaspoon freshly ground pepper
1 tablespoon chopped parsley

1) In a small bowl, cover the sun-dried tomatoes with hot tap water and let stand until they start to soften, about 20 minutes. Drain, slice, and set aside.

2) In a large saucepan, heat the oil over medium heat. Add the leeks, garlic, mushrooms, and sun-dried tomatoes. Cook, stirring occasionally, until the leeks are softened and translucent, about 5 minutes.

3) Add the barley, broth, and ¾ cup water. Bring to a boil and then reduce the heat to medium. Cook, uncovered, until the barley is tender but firm, about 30 minutes.

4) Reduce the heat to medium-low. Add the vermouth and 1½ cups water, ¼ cup at a time, stirring constantly, until the barley is creamy and the texture of a soupy stew, 5 to 10 minutes. Stir in the butter, Parmesan cheese, and pepper, mixing until creamy, 2 to 3 minutes. Serve in warm bowls, garnished with the parsley.

Collards and Rice

This dish is great slightly *sticky, almost a thick stew, so don't use converted or minute rice. For a more substantial version, add 1 (15-ounce) can of rinsed and drained black-eyed peas during the last five minutes of cooking.*

Makes 4 servings

1 small bunch of collard greens (about 1 pound)
½ tablespoon butter
1 tablespoon olive oil
3 large leeks (white and tender green), well rinsed and chopped

1 garlic clove, sliced
1½ cups long-grain white rice
1 (14½-ounce) can stewed tomatoes
1 (14½-ounce) can vegetable broth
Hot pepper sauce

1) To prepare the collard greens, remove the leaves from the thick stems. Discard the stems; rinse and dry the leaves, then chop very coarsely. They should measure about 6 cups.

2) In a large saucepan, melt the butter with the oil over medium heat. Add the leeks and garlic. Cook, stirring frequently, until the leeks start to brown, about 7 minutes.

3) Add the collard greens and toss until wilted, 3 to 5 minutes. Add the rice and stir to coat. Add the stewed tomatoes, broth, and ½ cup water. Bring to a boil; reduce the heat to low. Cover with waxed paper to seal well and then with the pan lid. Cook, stirring once, until the rice is tender and most of the liquid is absorbed, 18 to 20 minutes. Serve in warm bowls. Pass the hot sauce, so everyone can season it to their own taste.

Fresh Corn Salad with Cilantro Vinaigrette

While frozen corn makes a fine substitute in many dishes, fresh sweet corn turns this salad into a spectacular summer treat. When working with jalapeño peppers, use thin rubber gloves or, at the very least, wash your hands thoroughly after handling. **Makes 4 to 6 servings**

2 tablespoons red wine vinegar
1 to 2 small jalapeño peppers,
  seeded and minced
1 teaspoon Dijon mustard
¾ teaspoon salt
3 tablespoons vegetable oil
3 tablespoons chopped cilantro

7 ears of fresh corn
1 (14½-ounce) can black beans,
  rinsed and drained
2 plum tomatoes, chopped
2 scallions, chopped
1 small head of Boston lettuce,
  torn into bite-size pieces

1) In a large bowl, combine the red wine vinegar, jalapeño(s), mustard, and salt. Using a whisk or fork, slowly whisk in the oil until blended. Stir in the cilantro and set the dressing aside.

2) Fill a large saucepan with water. Bring to a rapid boil. Shuck the corn, remove the silk, and add the corn to the boiling water, breaking if necessary to fit. Cook until the corn is bright yellow but still crisp, 3 to 5 minutes. Drain or remove with tongs.

3) When the corn is cool enough to handle, cut the kernels off the cobs with a sharp knife. Add to the dressing and toss to mix. Add the beans, tomatoes, and scallions. Toss well.

4) Arrange the lettuce on a platter. Spoon the corn salad into the center. Serve at room temperature.

Curried Winter Vegetable Couscous

This is as close to instant curry *as you can get. Even children enjoy its flavor, and the condiments make this quick dish festive. If you are using canned vegetable broth, there is no need to add salt; but if you are using water, add ¾ teaspoon salt.*   ***Makes 4 servings***

1 tablespoon vegetable oil
1 small onion, chopped
1 tablespoon curry powder
1 garlic clove, minced
1 small head of broccoli, cut into
   1-inch florets (2 cups)
2 carrots, peeled and thinly
   sliced

1 plum tomato, chopped
1½ cups vegetable or chicken
   broth or water
1 cup couscous
1 cup plain yogurt
¼ cup chutney or raisins

1) In a large skillet, heat the oil over medium-low heat. Add the onion and cook, stirring frequently, until the onion is softened and translucent, about 3 minutes. Add the curry powder and cook, stirring, 1 minute longer.

2) Add the garlic, broccoli, carrots, tomato, and broth. Bring to a boil, cover, and cook until the broccoli is barely tender and just turns bright green, about 2 minutes.

3) Stir in the couscous. Immediately remove from the heat and let stand, covered for 10 minutes. Uncover, and fluff with a fork. Serve immediately, accompanied by the yogurt and chutney.

Saffron Couscous Salad

Saffron can be found in specialty food stores and health food stores. It adds lovely color and a subtle flavor, but it is admittedly expensive; so if you prefer, a pinch of turmeric can be used as a substitute. **Makes 6 servings**

⅓ cup fresh lemon juice
2 garlic cloves, minced
⅛ to ¼ teaspoon cayenne, to taste
⅓ cup olive oil
3¼ cups vegetable broth
¼ cup pine nuts or slivered almonds
Pinch of saffron
2 cups couscous
3 celery ribs, finely diced
¼ cup chopped fresh mint or flat-leaf parsley
¼ cup chopped scallions
¼ cup currants
Red or green leaf lettuce

1) In a small bowl, combine the lemon juice, garlic, and cayenne. With a small whisk or fork, gradually whisk in the olive oil. Stir in ¼ cup of the vegetable broth. Set the dressing aside.

2) In a dry medium saucepan, roast the nuts over medium heat, stirring constantly, until they start to smell aromatic but are not yet brown, about 3 minutes. Remove to a medium bowl.

3) Add the remaining 3 cups broth and the saffron to the saucepan. Bring to a boil. Stir in the couscous. Immediately remove from the heat, cover, and let stand until all the liquid is absorbed, 5 to 10 minutes.

4) Add the couscous, celery, mint, scallions, and currants to the bowl with the nuts. Fluff with a fork. Make a bed of lettuce on a small platter. Spoon the couscous onto the lettuce. Serve warm or at room temperature.

Steamed Eggplant with Sweet Pepper Relish

This is a light summer
alternative to fried eggplant. Serve with plenty of bread.

Makes 4 servings

2 medium eggplants (about
  1 pound each)
1 medium red bell pepper, cut
  into large wedges
1 medium yellow bell pepper, cut
  into large wedges
2 tablespoons chopped parsley
  plus sprigs for garnish
½ teaspoon grated fresh ginger

2 garlic cloves, minced
1 tablespoon red wine vinegar
1 teaspoon sugar
½ teaspoon salt
1 teaspoon Asian sesame oil
¼ teaspoon hot chili oil
¼ teaspoon freshly ground
  pepper

1) Pierce the eggplants 3 or 4 times with a fork. In a steamer pot large enough to hold 2 eggplants, over 2 inches rapidly boiling water, cook the eggplants, covered, until they are very soft, about 30 minutes.

2) Meanwhile, in a food processor, combine the bell peppers, chopped parsley, ginger, garlic, vinegar, sugar, ¼ teaspoon salt, sesame oil, and hot oil. Pulse until the peppers are coarsely chopped; do not puree.

3) While the eggplants are still warm, slice off the tops and quarter them lengthwise. Sprinkle with the remaining ¼ teaspoon salt and the pepper. Lay the eggplant sections out neatly on a plate or platter. Spoon the pepper relish over the eggplants. Garnish with parsley sprigs. Serve warm or at room temperature.

Fennel and Pea Risotto

This creamy Italian rice dish is usually served as a first course, but for vegetarians, it makes an elegant one-pot meal. Be sure to keep the risotto at a lively simmer, but not a full boil. If the heat is too high, the rice will be soft outside and hard inside. On the other hand, the rice should cook quickly enough to absorb the liquid and create a "rich," starchy sauce before the grains get mushy. **Makes 4 to 6 servings**

1 fennel bulb
2 tablespoons butter
1 tablespoon fruity olive oil
⅔ cup minced shallots
1½ cups Arborio rice
½ cup dry vermouth
2 garlic cloves, minced
½ teaspoon freshly ground pepper

¼ teaspoon fennel seeds
5 cups hot homemade vegetable or chicken broth or 3 (14½-ounce) cans vegetable broth mixed with 1½ cups water
1 cup fresh or frozen peas
½ cup grated Parmesan cheese
4 lemon wedges

1) Remove the outer stalks from the fennel bulb and discard. Trim the fennel and chop the bulb and frilly green ends. Set aside.

2) In a medium saucepan, melt the butter in the oil over medium heat. Add the shallots and cook, stirring frequently, until they are soft, 3 to 5 minutes. Add the fresh fennel, rice, vermouth, garlic, pepper, and fennel seeds. Cook, stirring frequently, until all the liquid is evaporated, about 2 minutes.

3) Add the broth ½ cup at a time, stirring constantly, until the rice absorbs the broth before making a new addition, about 2 minutes. When about 1 cup remains, stir in the peas. Add the last cup ¼ cup at a time.

4) As soon as you add the final ¼ cup broth, stir in ¼ cup of the Parmesan cheese and serve immediately in warm bowls, garnished with the fennel greens and lemon wedges. Pass the remaining cheese at the table.

Hummus with Steamed Vegetables

This version of hummus, a favorite Middle Eastern dish, is accompanied by steamed vegetables and pita. A colorful selection of vegetables is listed below, but almost any combination whether raw or cooked will work well with this recipe. ***Makes 3 to 4 servings***

4 pita breads, cut into wedges
1 (14½-ounce) can chickpeas (garbanzo beans), rinsed and drained
2 garlic cloves, minced
3 tablespoons tahini
¼ cup plain yogurt
3 tablespoons fresh lemon juice
½ teaspoon ground cumin
1 tablespoon extra-virgin olive oil

¼ teaspoon salt
⅛ teaspoon freshly ground pepper
1 cup large broccoli florets
1 cup large cauliflower florets
3 carrots, peeled and cut in half lengthwise and then on the diagonal into 2-inch pieces
1 pint cherry tomatoes
Lemon wedges

1) Preheat the oven to 275 degrees F. Wrap the pita breads in foil and place in the oven until warm, 10 to 15 minutes.

2) Meanwhile, in a food processor, combine the chickpeas, garlic, tahini, yogurt, lemon juice, cumin, olive oil, salt, and pepper. Puree until smooth, about 1 minute. Using a rubber spatula, remove to a small serving bowl.

3) Pour 2 inches of water into a large saucepan fitted with a steamer rack. Bring the water to a boil. Add the broccoli, cauliflower, and carrots to the steamer rack. Cover and cook over high heat for 5 minutes, or until the vegetables are crisp-tender.

4) To serve, set the bowl of hummus on a large platter. Using tongs, surround with the steamed vegetables, cherry tomatoes, and warm pita. Garnish with lemon wedges and serve.

Mediterranean Lentil-Olive Pâté

This flavorful puree of lentils and olives is superb when served with crusty French bread, sliced tomatoes, and bright green watercress. Lentils are found with the dried beans in the supermarket. Unlike many other legumes, they need no soaking, so you can make this dish on the spur of the moment. To keep the fat as low as possible, feel free to use nonfat yogurt here. ***Makes 4 to 6 servings***

1 cup dried lentils
½ teaspoon salt
½ cup pitted Calamata or oil-cured olives or ¼ cup black olive paste
1¼ cups plain yogurt
¼ cup extra-virgin olive oil
3 garlic cloves, crushed

3 tablespoons drained capers
¼ cup fresh lemon juice
1 baguette of French bread, sliced
2 medium tomatoes, sliced
1 bunch of watercress, tough stems trimmed
⅓ cup Niçoise olives

1) Rinse the lentils and pick over to remove any grit. Bring a large saucepan of water to a boil. Add the salt and the lentils. Cook until the lentils are soft, 30 to 35 minutes. Drain well.

2) In a food processor, puree the lentils, Calamata olives, ¼ cup of the yogurt, the olive oil, garlic, capers, and lemon juice until smooth. Pack the pâté into a small bowl lined with plastic wrap; press down to mold.

3) Invert the bowl onto a round platter to unmold the pâté. Carefully peel off the plastic wrap. Surround the pâté with the bread slices, tomatoes, and watercress. Garnish with the Niçoise olives. Pass the remaining yogurt on the side.

Warm Lentil Salad with Mixed Greens in Mustard Vinaigrette

For a special treat, try French *green lentils, available at gourmet shops; they hold their shape very well. For the greens, go for a mix of sweet and slightly bitter greens. Mixed baby lettuces and arugula or watercress would be my first choice. Romaine with shredded radicchio or Belgian endive would also be nice. Serve with chewy whole-grain bread.*

Makes 4 to 6 servings

1½ cups dried lentils
2 teaspoons salt
1 small red onion, chopped
4 teaspoons grainy mustard
2 garlic cloves, minced
3 tablespoons balsamic or red
    wine vinegar
½ teaspoon freshly ground
    black pepper

3 tablespoons olive oil
1 medium red bell pepper,
    chopped
¼ cup chopped parsley
2 to 3 cups loosely packed mixed
    salad greens
2 plum tomatoes, cut into
    wedges
⅓ cup crumbled feta cheese

1) In a large saucepan, bring 3 quarts of water to a boil. Add the lentils and cook for 20 to 30 minutes, until the lentils are softened but still have a little resistance in the center. Add 1 teaspoon of the salt and continue to cook until the lentils are tender but not falling apart, 5 to 10 minutes longer. Place the chopped red onion in a colander and drain the lentils over the onion to mellow its flavor. Transfer to a medium bowl.

2) While the lentils are cooking, combine the mustard, garlic, vinegar, black pepper, and remaining 1 teaspoon salt in a small bowl. Mix well. Slowly whisk in the oil until well blended. Pour the vinaigrette over the hot lentils. Add the bell pepper and parsley and toss to mix well.

3) Arrange the greens on a large platter. Spoon the lentils into the center. Arrange the tomato wedges around the rim. Sprinkle the feta cheese over the lentils and serve while they are still warm.

Sweet Pepper Pilaf with Broccoli and Black Beans

This flavorful and nutritious *bulgur dish may be served warm or cold. Sometimes I spoon it into bowls and other times into lettuce cups to be eaten out of hand.*
Makes 3 to 4 servings

1 cup small broccoli florets
1 small onion, coarsely chopped
1 red bell pepper, chopped
1 garlic clove, minced
1 tablespoon olive oil
Pinch of dried oregano
1 (8-ounce) can stewed tomatoes

1 cup coarse bulgur or cracked
  wheat
¾ teaspoon salt
⅛ teaspoon freshly ground
  pepper
¾ cup canned black beans,
  rinsed and drained

1) In a large saucepan of boiling salted water, cook the broccoli until crisp-tender but still bright green, 1 to 2 minutes. Drain and rinse briefly under cold running water; drain well.

2) In the same saucepan, combine the onion, bell pepper, garlic, oil, and oregano. Cook over medium heat, stirring frequently, until the onion is translucent, 3 to 5 minutes.

3) Stir in the tomatoes, bulgur, salt, pepper, and ¾ cup water. Bring to a boil, then reduce the heat to medium-low. Cover and cook until all the liquid is absorbed, 10 to 15 minutes.

4) Turn off the heat and stir in the broccoli and beans. Cover and let stand until the bulgur is tender but still slightly firm, 10 to 15 minutes. Serve warm or cold.

Potatoes Vinaigrette with Green, Yellow, and White Beans

I like to serve this on lettuce leaves, with a garnish of chopped olives—whatever kind I have on hand. A basket of chewy whole-grain bread would certainly not be amiss.

Makes 6 servings

2½ pounds red potatoes, scrubbed and cut into 1-inch pieces
6 ounces green beans, cut in half
6 ounces yellow wax beans, cut in half
7 sun-dried tomato halves, quartered lengthwise into thin strips
2 tablespoons red wine vinegar
2 garlic cloves, minced
3 tablespoons plus 1 teaspoon grainy mustard

1¼ teaspoons salt
1 teaspoon pepper
¼ cup extra-virgin olive oil
6 scallions, thinly sliced
¼ cup dry white wine or dry vermouth
¼ cup vegetable or chicken broth
1 (15-ounce) can cannellini beans, drained and well rinsed
Lettuce leaves

1) Fill a large saucepan fitted with a steamer with 1½ inches water. Add the potatoes, bring to a boil, and cook, covered, for 10 minutes. Add the green beans and wax beans; sprinkle the sun-dried tomatoes on top. Continue to cook until the potatoes and beans are tender but not mushy, 10 to 12 minutes. Transfer to a large serving bowl.

2) Meanwhile, in a small bowl, combine the vinegar, garlic, mustard, salt, and pepper. Whisk in the oil and stir in the scallions. Set the vinaigrette aside.

3) Pour the wine and broth over the hot vegetables. Toss gently to mix. Let stand for 5 minutes. Add the cannellini beans, pour on the vinaigrette, and gently toss again. Serve at room temperature.

Smashed Potatoes and Celery Root with Olive Oil and Chives

Celery root, also called celeriac, is a knobby root vegetable that is available in winter. It gives this light version of mashed potatoes its unique and satisfying flavor. Those who like the lumps in real mashed potatoes will love this dish of "smashed" potatoes and celery root topped with just a touch of fruity olive oil.

For a fancier topping, drizzle chive oil, rather than plain olive oil, on top. In a food processor, blend ¼ cup chopped chives with 1 cup olive oil. Strain. Drizzle 3 tablespoons of the chive oil over 4 servings. Garnish with 1 tablespoon additional chives. Reserve the remaining chive oil for another use.

Makes 4 to 6 servings

6 baking potatoes, peeled and cut into eighths
1 small celery root (¾ pound), peeled and cut into ½-inch pieces
1½ teaspoons butter
½ cup milk or vegetable broth

½ teaspoon salt
¼ teaspoon freshly ground pepper
3 tablespoons extra-virgin olive oil
2 tablespoons chopped chives or parsley

1) Fill a large saucepan fitted with a steamer with 1½ inches of water. Add the potatoes and celery root to the steamer rack. Bring the water to a boil, cover tightly, and cook, stirring once to rotate the vegetables, until they are soft, about 25 minutes.

2) In a large bowl, with a potato masher, smash the potatoes and celery root with the butter, milk, salt, and pepper, keeping them lumpy. Season with additional salt and pepper to taste.

3) Mound the smashed potatoes and celery root in 4 warm bowls. Drizzle with the olive oil and sprinkle with chives or parsley. Serve immediately.

Spaghetti Squash with Marinara Sauce

In this low-fat dish, the spaghetti-like strands of squash are a refreshing change from pasta. If you don't have a large enough pot to hold the two halves of the squash, it may be quartered or cooked in batches.

Makes 4 servings

1 spaghetti squash (about
 4 pounds)
1 tablespoon olive oil
1 small onion, chopped
2 garlic cloves, minced
1 tablespoon drained capers

1 (14½-ounce) can Italian-style
 stewed tomatoes
1 (8-ounce) can tomato sauce
1½ teaspoons butter
¼ teaspoon freshly ground pepper
Grated Parmesan cheese

1) Cut the squash lengthwise in half. Scrape out the seeds. In a saucepan large enough to hold the squash face down, bring 1 inch of water to a rapid boil. Place the squash, flesh down, in the water and cover. Steam until the squash can be flaked with a fork right down to the skin, 5 to 10 minutes. (Don't overcook or the squash will be mushy.) When the squash is done, remove with tongs and set aside until it is cool enough to handle.

2) Meanwhile, empty the pot of any remaining water. Set over medium heat and add the oil, onion, and garlic. Cook, stirring frequently to avoid burning, until the onion is softened and translucent, about 3 minutes. Stir in the capers and stewed tomatoes, crushing the tomatoes with a wooden spoon to break them into even smaller pieces. Add the tomato sauce, butter, and pepper. Bring to a boil, reduce the heat to medium-low, and simmer 5 minutes.

3) Using a fork, scrape the spaghetti-like strands of squash from the cavity of the squash into a large bowl. Make a well in the center and pour in the marinara sauce. Toss to coat. Pass a bowl of grated Parmesan cheese on the side.

Vegetable Fondue

Here cheese and chips are
transformed into an amusing vegetarian dinner where
everyone participates. Think of it as a fancy chile con queso.
Toasted French bread can be used to replace the tortilla chips.
For a party, this recipe is easily doubled or tripled.

Makes 3 to 4 servings

2 cups shredded Cheddar cheese
⅓ cup half-and-half
¼ cup spicy chunky-style salsa
1 chopped scallion
2 to 4 fresh jalapeño peppers, to
   taste, seeded and minced
4 medium red potatoes, cut into
   ¾-inch wedges

2 carrots, cut in half lengthwise,
   then crosswise into thirds
1 small head of broccoli, cut into
   1½-inch florets
2 celery ribs, cut in half
   lengthwise, then crosswise
   into thirds
Tortilla chips

1) In the top of a double boiler or in a medium stainless steel bowl, combine the cheese, half-and-half, salsa, scallion, and half the minced jalapeños. Mix well and set aside.

2) Fill a large saucepan fitted with a steamer rack with 2 inches of water. Place the potatoes on the steamer rack and bring the water to a boil over high heat. Cover and reduce the heat to medium. Cook for 10 minutes. Add the carrots and broccoli on top and cook for 5 minutes longer, until the potatoes are tender. Arrange the steamed vegetables on a large platter with the celery.

3) Set the double boiler or bowl on top of the saucepan over simmering water and cook, whisking occasionally, until the cheese is melted and the fondue is hot. Taste and add more jalapeño if you want. Transfer the dip to a warm bowl and serve immediately with the vegetables and tortilla chips.

Red Russian Vegetables with Dill and Caraway

his vegetarian feast, with its trio of warm winter salads, makes a gorgeous presentation on a large platter. I like to serve it with pumpernickel or whole-grain bread and a favorite cheese, such as Gruyère or Stilton. Be sure to pass cruets of oil and vinegar, so the diners can drizzle them on the lettuce if they choose. **Makes 4 servings**

1 bunch of beets (about 1 pound)
2 pounds red potatoes, cut into 2-inch pieces
1½ pounds cabbage, thinly sliced
1 head of red leaf lettuce
¼ cup sour cream
¼ teaspoon caraway seeds
1 teaspoon salt
½ teaspoon freshly ground pepper
1 tablespoon vegetable oil
1 tablespoon chopped fresh dill or 1 teaspoon dried
2 teaspoons grainy mustard
1½ tablespoons red wine vinegar
¼ cup diced red onion

1) Cut off both ends of the beets and peel them. Cut them into wedges, like a lemon, until the thickest part of each wedge is no more than ½ inch thick.

2) Fill a large saucepan fitted with a steamer rack with 1½ inches of water. Place the beets on one side of the steamer and the potatoes on the other side. Pile the cabbage on top of the potatoes.

3) Bring the water to a boil, cover, and cook over medium-high heat until both the potatoes and the beets are fork-tender, about 30 minutes.

4) Line a large platter with the lettuce leaves, with the frilly edge along the edge. In a medium bowl, using tongs, toss the cooked cabbage with 2 tablespoons sour cream, the caraway, ¼ teaspoon salt, and ¼ teaspoon pepper. Pile the cabbage on one-third of the platter, leaving the lettuce border.

5) Add the cooked potatoes to the same bowl and toss with the vegetable oil, remaining 2 tablespoons sour cream, the dill, mustard,

½ teaspoon salt, and the remaining ¼ teaspoon pepper. Place beside the potatoes. Add the beets to the bowl. Toss with the balsamic vinegar and the remaining ¼ teaspoon salt. Place beside the potatoes so the three salads form the shape of three large wedges in a pie, with the green running all around. Sprinkle the red onions on top and serve immediately.

Whole-Grain Pilaf with Tomato-Dill Relish

Wheatberries add slightly
*crunchy texture and nutty taste to this dish. They can be found
in health food stores. If you can't get them, simply omit them and
use an additional ¼ cup brown rice.*   ***Makes 4 to 6 servings***

1 tablespoon butter
2½ tablespoons olive oil
1 medium red onion, chopped
3 garlic cloves, minced
1¾ cups long-grain brown rice
¼ cup wheat or rye berries
1 (14½-ounce) can vegetable
  broth
¼ teaspoon salt

¼ teaspoon freshly ground pepper
4 large plum tomatoes, chopped
2½ tablespoons chopped fresh dill
4 teaspoons grainy mustard
4 teaspoons chopped capers
4 teaspoons fresh lemon juice
¼ pound sugarsnap peas,
  strings removed

1) In a medium saucepan, melt the butter in 1 tablespoon of the oil over
medium heat. Add the red onion and garlic and cook, stirring occasionally,
until the onion starts to brown, 5 to 7 minutes.

2) Add the brown rice and wheatberries, stirring to coat with oil. Add
the vegetable broth, salt, pepper, and 2¼ cups water. Bring to a boil;
reduce the heat to medium-low. Cover and cook until the liquid is absorbed,
35 to 40 minutes.

3) While the grains are cooking, make the relish. In a small bowl,
combine the remaining 1½ tablespoons oil with the tomatoes, dill,
mustard, capers, and lemon juice. Toss to mix well. Season with additional
salt and pepper to taste.

4) When the pilaf is finished, remove from the heat, pour the sugarsnap peas on top, cover, and let stand for 3 minutes, or until they are bright
green and warmed through. Serve the pilaf and peas in warm bowls,
accompanied by the tomato-dill relish.

Wild and Brown Rice Salad in Lettuce Cups

Unlike traditional steamed rice, wild and brown rice here are cooked like pasta, in plenty of boiling water to separate the grains and prevent stickiness.

Makes 4 servings

½ cup wild rice
1 cup brown rice
2 carrots, peeled and finely diced
2 celery ribs, finely diced
1 garlic clove, minced
2 tablespoons red wine vinegar
1½ teaspoons Dijon mustard
¼ teaspoon salt
¼ teaspoon freshly ground pepper

3 tablespoons olive oil
2 scallions, sliced
¼ cup golden raisins
1 head of Boston lettuce, separated into leaves
2 tablespoons toasted sunflower seeds

1) In a large saucepan of boiling salted water, cook the wild rice for 5 minutes. Add the brown rice and cook until the rice is just tender but still slightly chewy, about 40 minutes. Add the carrots and celery to the pot. Immediately drain well in a colander, shaking to remove any excess water.

2) While the rice is cooking, make the vinaigrette: In a small bowl, combine the garlic, vinegar, mustard, salt, and pepper. Whisk in the olive oil until well blended.

3) In a large bowl, toss the warm wild and brown rice with the vinaigrette. Stir in the scallions and raisins. Season with additional salt and pepper to taste. Arrange the lettuce leaf cups upright on plates or platters. Spoon the rice salad into the leaves and sprinkle the sunflower seeds on top.

Index

Polenta, beans puttanesca on, 67
Portobello mushroom(s)
  lasagna, 139
  steaks, marinated, 48
Potato(es)
  and celery root with olive oil
    and chives, smashed, 171
  and eggplant curry, 70
  and leek soup, 30
  and parsnip fritters with apple
    horseradish cream, 51
  red
    and cheese pizza, 142
    and creamy spinach stew,
      73
    sweet and sour cabbage
      with raisins and, 112
  and rutabaga gratin, 144
  stuffed with cottage cheese
    and scallions, dinner
    baked, 143
  vinaigrette with green, yellow,
    and white beans, 170
  Yukon gold, and sorrel stew
    with sweet corn, 79
Pudding
  corn, savory, with tomato
    salsa, 132
  whole wheat bread, with broc-
    coli and Cheddar, 150
Puttanesca, beans, on polenta,
  67

Quesadillas, bean and avocado, 35
Quick black bean chili with
  goat cheese, 63
Quinoa
  soup with córn, 21
  stir-fry, lemon-soy, 118

Radiatore with summer tomato sauce, 92
Raisins, sweet and sour cabbage with potatoes and,
  112
Ramen noodles
  in bok choy and browned on-
    ions with broken noo-
    dles, 108
  in wokked noodles with spin-
    ach and mushrooms, 116
Ravioli
  with lemon-herb butter, 93
  soup, ricotta wonton, 22
Red bean(s)

and acorn squash chili, 62
and avocado quesadillas, 35
Red bell peppers. *See* Pep-
  per(s), sweet bell
Red lentil and rice stew with
  cauliflower and peas, 72
Red onion and asparagus frittata, 34
Red potato and creamy spinach
  stew, 73
Red Russian vegetables with
  dill and caraway, 174
Relish
  sweet pepper, steamed egg-
    plant with, 164
  tomato-dill, whole-grain pilaf
    with, 176
Rice. *See also* Risotto
  collards and, 160
  and red lentil stew with cauli-
    flower and peas, 72
  salad, wild and brown, in let-
    tuce cups, 177
Ricotta wonton ravioli soup, 22
Risotto
  barley, with wild mushrooms
    and sun-dried tomatoes,
    159
  fennel and pea, 165
Roasted pepper and arugula
  stromboli, 128
Romano cheese, penne and
  broccoli rabe with, 91
Rosemary vegetables, roasted,
  148
Rutabaga and potato gratin, 144

Saffron
  couscous salad, 163
  soup, spring, 23
Salad
  avocado and goat cheese,
    warm, with spicy lime-to-
    mato dressing, 152
  corn, fresh, with cilantro vin-
    aigrette, 161
  maifun noodle, crispy, 114
  escarole, with warm pears,
    blue cheese, and wal-
    nuts, 45
  falafel, with tahini dressing,
    46
  of field greens with roasted
    garlic and goat cheese
    croutons, 153

red Russian vegetables with
  dill and caraway, 174
saffron couscous, 163
tortellini, summer, 98
vegetables à la Grecque, 77
lentil, with mixed greens in
  mustard vinaigrette,
  warm, 168
wild and brown rice, in lettuce cups, 177
greens with Gorgonzola
  croutons, wilted, 106
zucchini Niçoise, 80
Salsa
  Mexican, fusilli with, 88
  tomato
    corn pudding, savory, with,
      132
    fresh, Mexican eggs in, 41
    -ginger, zucchini and carrots
      with, 124
Sandwiches, seared eggplant,
  with sesame mayonnaise,
  42
Santa Fe stir-fry with squash,
  sweet peppers, and corn,
  119
Satay sauce, tempeh burgers
  with, 52
Sauce
  black bean, broccoli stir-fry
    with, 109
  blueberry, cottage cheese pan-
    cakes with, 44
  cider maple, whole wheat cin-
    namon French toast with
    raisins and, 56
  lentil, fusilli with, 87
  marinara, spaghetti squash
    with, 172
  morel, creamy, fresh fettuc-
    cine with, 86
  peanut, Indonesian green
    beans and tofu in, 71
  satay, tempeh burgers with, 52
  tomato
    lemony, chickpeas with, 69
    marinara, spaghetti squash
      with, 172
    smoky, Go-West wagon
      wheels with, 100
    summer, radiatore with, 92
  sun-dried, corn cakes with, 37
  tsaziki, cashew croquettes
    with, 38

tomato and escarole, 74
vegetable curry, spicy South Indian, 75
vegetable goulash, 76
vegetables à la Grecque, 77
yam and wild mushroom, 78
Yukon gold potato and sorrel, with sweet corn, 79
zucchini Niçoise, 80
Stir-fry. *See also* Wok dishes
broccoli, with black bean sauce, 109
green bean, 113
lemon-soy quinoa, 118
lemon-soy vegetable, 121
Santa Fe, with squash, sweet peppers, and corn, 119
Vietnamese vegetable, 123
Stock, vegetable, 20
Stromboli, arugula and roasted pepper, 128
Strudel, spinach and feta, 146
Succotash, bulgur, 111
Summer harvest casserole, 138
Summer tortellini salad, 98
Sun-dried tomato(es)
barley risotto with wild mushrooms and, 159
pesto, spaghetti with roasted peppers and, 96
sauce, corn cakes with, 37
Surprise vegetable almondine, 122
Sweet and sour cabbage with potatoes and raisins, 112
Sweet corn, Yukon gold potato and sorrel stew with, 79
Swiss chard and butternut squash stew, 68
Szechuan cold sesame noodles, 101

Tahini dressing, falafel salad with, 46
Tamari, barley and shiitake stew with ginger and, 66
Tempeh burgers with satay sauce, 52
Teriyaki tofu on buckwheat noodles with watercress, 102
Texas tortilla pie, 145
Tofu
and green beans in peanut sauce, Indonesian, 71

mushroom braised, with snow peas, 117
teriyaki, on buckwheat noodles with watercress, 102
Tomato(es)
-dill relish, whole-grain pilaf with, 176
-garlic vinaigrette, penne and asparagus with, 90
-lime dressing, spicy, warm avocado and goat cheese salad with, 152
pesto, sun-dried, spaghetti with roasted peppers and, 96
salsa
-ginger, zucchini and carrots with, 124
Mexican eggs in fresh, 41
savory corn pudding with, 132
sauce
lemony, chickpeas with, 69
marinara, spaghetti squash with, 172
summer, radiatore with, 92
sun-dried, corn cakes with, 37
wagon wheels, Go-West, with smoky, 100
soup
gazpacho, dinner, 13
Italian roasted red pepper and, 19
with orzo and Parmesan cheese, 24
stew, escarole and, 74
stuffed with eggplant, Moroccan, 54
sun-dried
barley risotto with wild mushrooms and, 159
pesto, spaghetti with roasted peppers and, 96
sauce, corn cakes with, 37
Tortellini salad, summer, 98
Tortilla(s)
Brie, and fresh mango chutney, 50
pie, Texas, 145
Tsaziki sauce, cashew croquettes with, 38

Vegetable(s)
aioli, grand, 134
à la Grecque, 77

almondine, surprise, 122
battered, with lime, 120
cobbler, 149
couscous, curried winter, 162
curry, spicy South Indian, 75
fondue, 173
goulash, 76
pesto gnocchi with, 89
red Russian, with dill and caraway, 174
roasted rosemary, 148
steamed, hummus with, 166
stir-fry
lemon-soy, 121
Vietnamese, 123
Vermicelli with cilantro pesto, 99
Vietnamese vegetable stir-fry, 123
Vinaigrette
cilantro, fresh corn salad with, 161
garlic-tomato, penne and asparagus with, 90
mustard, warm lentil salad with mixed greens in, 168
orange-sesame, asparagus and couscous with, 158
potatoes, with green, yellow, and white beans, 170

Wagon wheel pasta with smoky tomato sauce, Go-West, 100
Walnuts, escarole salad with warm pears, blue cheese, and, 45
Warm avocado and goat cheese salad with spicy lime-tomato dressing, 152
Warm lentil salad with mixed greens in mustard vinaigrette, 168
Watercress
soup, wild rice and, 28
teriyaki tofu on buckwheat noodles with, 102
White bean(s)
artichoke, and fennel ambrosia, Italian, 65
and kale soup, Spanish, 27
potatoes vinaigrette with green, yellow, and, 170
White hominy grits 'n eggs, 47